MW00526204

When souls awaken

Real-Life Accounts of Past-Life and Life-Between-Lives Regressions

When souls awaken

Real-Life Accounts of Past-Life and
Life-Between-Lives Regressions

Pieter Elsen

Copyright © 2019 Pieter Elsen
ALL RIGHTS RESERVED

* *

Title: **When Souls Awaken - Real-Life Accounts of Past-Life and Life-Between-Lives Regressions**

ISBN 13: 978-1-7352856-0-3

Library of Congress Control Number: 2019911136

****

FOR MORE INFORMATION

If you wish to learn in greater detail about the teachings in this book, please email us at elsenhypnotherapy@gmail.com

For information on our Books, Audio and Video visit:
www.elsenhypnotherapy.com
www.whensoulsawaken.com

****

Printed in the USA

TABLE OF CONTENTS

Acknowledgments		7
Preface		9
Introduction		11
SECTION 1		15
1	Why it helps to remember	19
2	Knowing the nature of the soul	35
3	Seeking integration	51
4	The ways of higher consciousness	69
5	Awakening	81
6	Living free	97
SECTION 2		111
7	Living the enlightened life	115
8	The higher purpose of grief and loss	135
9	You are not crazy	153
10	Shifting the paradigm	167
11	Freedom	187
SECTION 3		207
12	The fourth state	211
13	Beyond the waves of the mind	223
14	Understanding the nature of duality	243
15	The wisdom of the awakened ones	259
16	Re-connecting to our divine purpose	289
CONCLUSION		311
17	Climbing the mountain	313
	About the author	329

Acknowledgments

This book wouldn't have come into existence without the continuous support of my dearest wife and best friend Jenna. Her encouragement, inspiration, and divine personality are the light of my life.

I would also like to thank my dear friend Cayenne Graves for proofreading and editing this book. I couldn't have found anybody better suited for this work than you.

Last but not least I feel blessed to pay homage to the source of my inspiration, Dr. Michael Newton, whose works 'Journey of Souls' and 'Destiny of Souls' has not only inspired me, but millions with me to dive deeper into the mysteries of our souls, traveling through many lifetimes, to discover the true nature of our Self unfolding within.

Preface

This is a book about the nature of the soul. I will be presenting cases of real-life clients who entered higher states of consciousness during Past Life and Life Between Lives Spiritual Regressions. The incredible accounts of their journey through countless lifetimes, and their observations, while they were beyond the body in a superconscious state, are too amazing not to share.

I do this work for a living. I travel around the country to see people interested in their past lives, and who are particularly interested in the in-between lives state. You may not be all too familiar with this concept, but the life-between-lives spiritual regression techniques were pioneered by Dr. Michael Newton. His work has changed my life.

In his books 'Journey of Souls' and 'Destiny of Souls' Dr. Michael Newton presents his discoveries and shares hundreds of cases of the life-between-lives regressions he conducted with his clients.

This book attempts to start where he left off. In it, I present some of the spiritual realizations and explanations that a new generation of awakened souls have experienced. The times have changed. More knowledge is available than even 30 or 40 years ago when Dr. Newton first wrote these books. People have changed and evolved at an incredible pace. The collective unconscious has adapted ideas from oriental philosophy and different spiritual traditions and especially in the United States this has contributed to a new way of thinking among many.

I hope that this work may be a welcome contribution to the spiritual community of sincere seekers, who are ready to receive in their lives the highest states of spiritual awakening.

Introduction

There are a number of books out there today that delve into the concept of reincarnation. Brian Weiss with 'Many Lives, Many Masters' and Michael Newton with the 'Journey (and Destiny) of Souls' are two of the more famous examples. These great groundbreaking therapists were pioneers who have helped us get acquainted with the ideas of rebirth and life after death. Ideas that needed time to be accepted in a predominantly Christian-Judaic culture.

Accordingly, these therapists were initially hesitant to share their findings. Michael Newton, for example, waited decades to present his work. They were not only concerned about their own reputation in the academic world but also cautious not to offend established religious sentiments.

The burden of academia can be a heavy load to carry. Concerns about our reputation can make us hold back. This is equally true trying to accommodate the feelings we as a society hold dear about life and death. Brian Weiss, Michael Newton and many others of that era were subjected to the pressures of academia and religious sentiments. From their background and standpoint, it took a certain amount of courage to publish their findings. Thankfully their work was received positively.

It is really not that surprising. When we accept the idea of the soul and reincarnation, we are responding to the verity of our own true identity. It strikes a chord within us. There is a recognition of the truth of our own Self buried beneath centuries of forgetfulness and struggles.

We now live in a different world. The pioneers in this field felt they had to make their case for reincarnation. Academics like Raymond Moody and Dr. Ian Stephenson dedicated decades of their lives trying to present evidence of life after death and reincarnation. We are grateful.

Unburdened by societal resistance and the need to convince, we now live in a different time. Millions of immigrants have carried with them their Oriental belief systems. TV and the internet have exposed us to knowledge our ancestors never dreamt of. We now live in a world where Yoga has become a household name and where ideas like Guru and Karma are living and breathing realities.

So this is not going to be a book that attempts to convince you of the truth of reincarnation. We are beyond that. If you don't believe in it that's ok. This book is for those who feel the need to go deeper into understanding the nature of the soul, why we reincarnate and the purpose of it all. As I share with you cases of clients and their remarkable journey through many lifetimes, the wisdom and sensitivity of their souls will leave you in awe. There is so much to learn from their travels through time, and their contact with a higher consciousness in-between-lives.

I, for one, remember some of my past lives. As a kid, I had vivid dreams of my time as a soldier during the French Revolution and my time in India as a spiritual aspirant. I consciously remember the time before I took this birth, where I was standing looking down at life accompanied by my guide, eager to start life all over again.

So, for me personally, rebirth is a reality. From my early childhood, I tried to make sense of this reality and, how knowing this affected every decision I made. I was lucky to have parents who supported this kind of thinking, leaving me free to philosophize and experiment. It is no wonder then that at the age of twenty-three after I finished college, I joined a religious order near Paris to become a monk in an Eastern tradition.

I spent the next twenty-one years living the monks' life.

Eleven of those I spent in India where I visited the places of my last birth. When decades later I happened upon the books of Dr. Michael Newton I realized that this was the work I was destined to do. It was during this time that I met my twin soul, Jenna, with whom I have lived many lives before. Together we set out on a soul journey that leads us here today, sharing with you my discoveries about life, death and our true identity as souls.

As a professional regressionist, I see clients that come to me for past-life and life-between-lives regression sessions every day. I have conducted hundreds of sessions with people of all kinds. I feel it is profoundly important to share with you what I have learned from all these amazing souls. With their permission and to protect the identity of my clients I have changed their names. Their accounts in these chapters are verbatim transcripts of the sessions. I will be sharing with you real client testimonials of their lives in different bodies and their experience as souls beyond this body. I will also share with you my thoughts about these cases and further elaborate on the nature of our soul.

Due to my rather unusual personal history, I've been in the presence of some truly remarkable awakened souls. Throughout this book, I share with you some of my encounters with them.

May this inspire you, may this awaken you, and may this make you love your true Self even more.

Pieter

Section 1

Insights For Self-Discovery Through
Understanding One's Past

This book is divided into three distinct sections.

Section 1 of this book focuses on the relationship between Past-Life Regression and Life-Between-Lives Regression, and how this therapeutic combination is extremely effective in helping us understand our purpose here on earth and beyond.

Section 1 is also an introduction to the concept of consciousness, and what entering higher states of consciousness means for our 'normal' state of consciousness in our regular day-to-day life.

Section 2 *is dedicated to understanding the three fundamental pillars of our lives. Through the accounts of those who have entered the life-between-lives states, we learn how to best live a balanced life. One that is not only helping us achieve the maximum amount of happiness here and now, but one that also is in tune with our overall divine purpose.*

Section 3 *is comprised of accounts of those that have become awakened to their highest purpose. They describe what it is like to experience high states of consciousness and share with us their accounts of spiritual awakening. Their experiences are a source of inspiration and paint a picture of what awaits all of us when we wake up to our true Selves.*

Chapter 1
Why It Helps To Remember

I would like to start by presenting a most interesting case. Marie is a young successful 27-year-old business woman. In her pre-session questionnaire, she mentioned her struggle to fit in with society, with the apparent need to socialize, get married and have kids. She greatly doubts herself and her capacity to do what she feels society demands of her, expressing her conflict between how she really feels inside and what life around her expects of her.

This first case I share here is important for several reasons. First and foremost, it is a beautiful example of somebody who needed to remember her past. Marie in her normal day-to-day conscious state did not remember her past. Surely, she accepted the idea of reincarnation, but it wasn't a living and breathing reality. Remembering her past, having this experience herself, allowed her to make more sense of the struggles and tendencies she was living with today and helped her shape a new plan for the future.

As we travel back in time the scene opens up somewhere in a remote desert, long, long ago.

P: Can you describe what you see around you?

Marie: (*soft voice*) I'm in the desert. It's peaceful here.

P: Is it day or night?

Marie: It's night.

P: Are you a man or a woman?

Marie: A woman.

P: What is the first thing you notice?

Marie: It's so peaceful. I'm looking up at the stars.

P: What are you doing out here at night?

Marie: This is where I stay.

P: You live here?

Marie: Yes.

P: Tell me more.

Marie: I like my solitude. I came here to be alone.

P: What makes you want to be alone?

Marie: I like to contemplate, think, meditate. You need to be alone for this.

P: How does this make you feel?

Marie: It's hard to describe the peace and joy I experience (*emotional*).

When I progress her forward in time we suddenly find ourselves in another lifetime as a mother of 2 kids in a suburban house. It's unusual during a regression to jump forward into another life, especially when the client simultaneously retains an awareness of the previous life we just visited. My first task is to check whether or not the client has lost hypnotic depth and is starting to mix conscious memories with past life memories. But this soon turns out not to be the case.

P: Describe what is happening now?

Marie: I'm at home.

P: Can you describe the setting to me?

Marie: It's suburbia. Quite modern. I don't like it here.

P: What don't you like about it?

Marie: (*sobbing*) It's not like the desert. The bondage, the kids.

P: Tell me more about how you feel?

Marie: I remember my life in the desert. The freedom, the meditations. I can't do that here. I've lost my peace. I've lost my connection. It's terrible. I hate this life.

P: Why are we here now? Why this memory?

Marie: I need to see this. The consequence of my actions. And what happens to me when I allow myself to get too much involved in the world. It grabs you. It devours you.

She continues describing her life in what seems to be a life before her current life as Marie. I soon ask her to return back to her life in the desert, but this time forward in time to another relevant moment in her life as a desert hermit.

P: What is happening right now?

Marie: I'm not alone anymore.

P: Who is there with you?

Marie: Others have moved here too.

P: When you say others, you mean family, friends?

Marie: No, just people.

P: Just a few or many?

Marie: Just a few.

P: What are they doing here?

Marie: They like to live like me.

P: What's your relationship with them?

Marie: I don't have much of a relationship with them. They leave me alone.

P: How do you feel about that?

Marie: It's ok.

P: Does it bother you they are here now?

Marie: Not really. Actually, I don't mind their company.

P: You don't?

Marie: Not really.

We move forward in time to when she is considerably older and the story continues:

P: Can you tell me what is happening now?

Marie: I'm hungry.

P: Isn't there enough to eat?

Marie: No. We don't have enough resources.

P: Is it because you are in the desert?

Marie: No, it has always been able to provide. There are too many people now. We're thinking about moving.

P: Who's we?

Marie: The elders.

P: Are you one of the elders?

Marie: Yes. But I'm not much involved. I don't want to go.

P: Why not?

Marie: I love it here. I just like to help.

P: Tell me more about that?

Marie: I try to help those in need. Give them my food. The hungry, the needy.

P: What makes you do that?

Marie: I've come to like the people. I need to help.

P: What about you wanting to be alone?

Marie: Yes, I still like to be alone. But I've learned.

P: What did you learn?

Marie: To share, to be with others.

P: So no more lonely contemplation then?

Marie: No I never said that. It's a middle path. Don't get too involved. Stay at the edge of the community, but stay involved. Stay connected.

P: Why is that important to you?

Marie: (*tears running down her cheeks*) It's important to love, to give, to share. But you also need to spend time alone. Time to be with the desert, with the stars. Stay connected with that as well.

As we move to her death and her reflections on the life she just lived, she described how she died of starvation due to a lack of resources.

P: What do you think about the life you just lived?

Marie: It was great. I was happy.

P: How do you feel about your death?

Marie: I don't mind. I was happy to give my life so that even one soul could live.

P: That's quite a departure from that woman who came alone to the desert.

Marie: Not really. I like to be alone. I need to be alone. But I learned to give. To care, to connect. That's important too. Important for my soul.

P: What is the most important lesson you learned?

Marie: That we need to strike a balance. That there is no need to give up aloneness. As a matter of fact, for me, that's what I need most and what I like most. It's ok to be alone. It's ok to live and choose a life that allows you to be alone. But that in order to feed the heart you also need to connect to others and give. But one does not need to be at the expense of the other.

From here we went to the life-between-lives state. Here we could talk about all the lives she had lived with objectivity and understanding.

Past life regression provides context. A place where we can discover the origin of certain tendencies that we still carry with us today. You would think that our past has been one where we lived a much more primitive kind of existence. In a certain way that is true, especially technologically. But when it comes to the internal experiences of souls that is not always the case. Often souls have already developed certain qualities that in this life are either buried or latent.

Conflicts arise in this life when deep inside, the soul craves for or subconsciously remembers the life it has lived and it is currently not able to recreate the circumstances that allow these qualities to shine. A past life regression can help to expose these qualities reminding the soul that these qualities have already been developed.

The life between life stage takes this realization to a whole new level where the comparison between the current and past life can begin. Here we can also get in touch with the intentions the soul has set before it took this birth.

P: Is this a good time to talk about your hermit life and your current life?

Marie: Yes, I'm ok now.

P: When we compare your life as a hermit with this current life as Marie, what are your thoughts?

Marie: I was more connected as a hermit.

P: Connected how?

Marie: Well, I knew what my purpose was and what made me happy. I was clear and strong in my ways.

P: And today as Marie that is not the case?

Marie: Life is different nowadays. Society is different. The demands are different.

P: Help me understand.

Marie: It doesn't seem to be alright to want to be alone. I like to be alone.

P: Who exactly says you can't be alone?

Marie: Well, I have been thinking as Marie that it's not ok to be alone.

This is where the transformative aspect of the life-between-lives experience becomes manifest. She now is neither identified as Marie (her current life) nor with her life as a hermit. She has dropped any and all identifications with her conditioning as Marie. Conditioning that incarnating into a body projects upon the soul.

Once a soul drops even momentarily, the conditioning of family, environment, body and the collective subconscious, it gains an incredible clarity.

P: Please tell me more.

Marie: I see now that as Marie I should be more confident to express my need to be alone. That's it's not weird. That as Marie I need to design and organize my life in such a way that I spend more time alone.

P: Is she not doing that now? (*I'm now using the pronoun 'she' to further help her objectify her observations and she immediately detaches more from Marie*).

Marie: She struggles. She is too much involved with the world and too much concerned about its approval.

P: Help me understand.

Marie: Rather than realizing that it's ok to not want to have a bunch of kids and get caught up into that kind of life, she needs to remember that it's possible to live life in such a way that she can have both. Both human connection and alone time.

P: Is that why we had the glimpse of that life as a housewife?

Marie: Yes, she needed to remember the bondage. Or rather that for somebody like me who needs alone time, that kind of life won't work.

P: Ok, so kindly summarize this for me.

Marie: Summarize what?

P: Your observation as a soul, about Marie and the hermit's way of life.

Marie: As a soul I need balance. As a hermit, I already attained a great deal of balance. In the life as Marie, I need to integrate this balance even more. Take it to the next level.

P: What do you mean with 'take it to the next level'?

Marie: It's not about just repeating what I already did. I took this birth as Marie to further my development.

P: What does that development look like?

Marie: It's about my overall purpose. As a soul, I need to achieve freedom. Marie needs to become awake to this fact. Not to allow the conditions of her life to make her forget what she contemplated as a hermit. You live in the world but you don't become the world.

P: How can she do that?

Marie: Today is a start. A reminder.

P: That's good to hear.

Marie: She needs to meditate more. She also needs to become aware that's it's ok to be in a relationship as long as that relationship allows her that freedom. It can't tie her down.

P: Isn't this paradoxical?

Marie: Not if lived with awareness. She needs to find a partner in life that understands her purpose. And that his purpose is aligned with hers. And that purpose for Marie is the attainment of higher consciousness and to gain internal freedom. It would only be a paradoxical situation if she goes into a relationship randomly and expects a regular guy to comprehend this. Then it's better to be alone in the desert.

P: Understood haha.

Marie: Yes. Marie needs to realize that's it's better to be alone and happy than allow herself to be indoctrinated by the wants and culture of the society around her.

P: So you're saying she needs to be strong, awake and patient?

Marie: Exactly. She can wait until the right person comes along. She can have both. Living an enlightened life in freedom and have an intimate connection with a partner and even the people around her.

It is common that as the session progresses the soul becomes increasingly authoritative. It starts to gain tremendous clarity. It becomes increasingly aware of its higher purpose and its soul identity and wants to clearly communicate that to its embodied Self.

P: What about these people around her?

Marie: She's been struggling with that. Her work demands her to be around people. She's uncomfortable with that.

P: What do you advise?

Marie: The same thing. To walk the middle path. She doesn't need to be afraid to mix with people.

P: Afraid?

Marie: Yes, she's been afraid only because she hasn't found an inner balance. Once she accepts that it is ok to be alone she'll lose that fear.

P: Help me understand.

Marie: The alone time will allow her to become centered. It's what she needs. She should stop being apologetic about that or repress that need. When she embraces it and makes it a part of her life she'll gain tremendous balance and strength.

P: And that will allow her to deal with her fear of mixing with others?

Marie: Yes. Once you are centered nothing can shake you. From that centered awareness she can freely mix with others without losing herself. It's when you are not centered, not in touch with your own soul and its purpose, that you get lost or intimidated.

P: I see. So when she is aware of who she is and stays true to that awareness, other people's energy won't affect her.

Marie: Yes. Though it's not so much other people's energies that affect her. Her reluctance to mix freely with others stems from her lack of centeredness. She hasn't listened to her need to be alone, though she craves it, and feels perpetually off center. Mixing with other people only accentuates that need. Today she is reminded of the bliss and happiness her desert life gave her. From now onwards, when she starts to listen to her need to contemplate and accepts that fact that it is ok to have that need, things will change. She will gain strength and happiness from these meditations. With that internal strength and happiness, she can go out and mix. You understand now?

P: Yes, I understand. It's a lesson we could all learn.

Marie: True. We get too much identified with the body and the temporary roles we play. We forget we're an eternal soul destined to be free.

P: What is your final advice for Marie

Marie: Meditate. It's how she stays connected with her true identity. All troubles start when she forgets that and gets identified with this current incarnation. We're eternally free.

I clearly remember tossing restlessly in my bed at the age of 14 years old. Every night I lay there pondering the questions of life and death. My main concern was, why am I here? Why here in Holland in this affluent family, in this affluent country? Why here? It concerned me. How come others don't have these opportunities? How come others do better? For me, the only reason to account for all of these differences was the idea of reincarnation. It had to be so. I was here, now, due to the result of everything I had done before. My body, my parents, my country, the degree of possibilities laid out before me, all of this, was the result of my past and was designed to help me on my way.

Even at that young age, it made me aware that I had a responsibility towards myself. A responsibility to create circumstances that would allow me to further this development and not bind myself with careless karmic actions that I would have to undo later on. You can say that this realization made me somewhat cautious. It took me a long time to transform this kind of thinking into actual inner freedom. But more of that later.

Another beautiful finding in Marie's case is her awareness of her true Self, her true free and eternal identity beyond the body. Her own higher Self is helping Marie get reacquainted with this idea and give her the courage and strength to see beyond the limitations of the world she lives in.

The notion of reincarnation is tied to two philosophical ideas, that of the eternal nature of the soul and the idea of karma. You can't have reincarnation without a soul and without a karmic law that governs these rebirths. These concepts are tied together.

It is true that we will have a hard time scientifically proving this. It doesn't matter. It reminds me of a tribe I visited deep inside the jungles of India. Amidst the large trees, deep inside a rock formation, the tribe had built a nature shrine with a large stone as the centerpiece. Beneath it was a carving that translated: 'If you believe this is a rock, it is a rock. If you believe it is God, it is God'.

There comes a time in our lives that we lose the inclination to argue. Instead, we seek from our own experience something that can help us move forward. So rather than trying to justify what we already know to be true, even if many around us don't share these beliefs, we long for and seek a soul connection. As if in the depths of our minds, like a faint echo in our subconscious mind, the memory of our past lives and the life-between-life as a free soul pushes us to reawaken this experience in the here and now.

So I don't like to argue about these subjects. I can present to you here a lengthy thesis about the reasons why you should believe in reincarnation. But if some believe it is a rock it will always be a rock for them. I respect the fact that many will think this way. If you are like me and have always been looking for your own answers instead of seeking other's approval, you can ask yourself; is this helpful to me?

I have taken the idea of soul, karma, and rebirth as the fundamental pillars of my life. The wisdom and depth of understanding coming from the beautiful souls who have realized this reality for themselves are important to share. They have found that this experience has really helped them find purpose and meaning and their insights can help us do the same.

Chapter 2

Knowing The Nature Of The Soul

It is a question that many of us ask ourselves, what is the nature of the soul? How does it reincarnate and where is it when not embodied? What does it look like? Sometimes during a life-between-lives regression session, I am allowed the opportunity to ask these questions on behalf of the client when a soul is particularly talkative, willing and capable.

This particular client, John, is a middle-aged self-employed gentleman interested in the nature of the soul. In his day-to-day life, he's a meditator with many interesting spiritual experiences. What is unique about this session is that it allows us to witness a soul that is able to express itself in such lucid and clear terms, able to speak from the highest levels of consciousness.

As we move through one of his past lives as a native American, he vividly describes his walk on the Trail of Tears and the terrible forced relocations he and his people had to endure. His detailed and emotional accounts are heartbreaking and he is visibly moved by the loss of his way of life. He had been a peaceful hunter who was happy with his people and his spiritually attuned way of life. After we move through the death scene and ascend to the life-between-lives world, we are able to talk about the nature of the soul.

P: What is this place?

John: It's not so much a place as a state, a frequency.

P: Can you explain that to me?

John: It's not that I'm 'somewhere', like a location. It's more that I feel I'm right here with you but at a much higher reality. As if our worlds coexist, but at different frequencies.

P: So you are here now?

John: Yes and no. The body is there with you and I'm aware of you. But my true Self is at a different frequency, in a different place. In a non-physical sense.

P: What does this feel like? Can you describe this to me?

John: It's like my awareness is light. It's not physical. It's consciousness without the burden of the body. I feel blissful and awake.

P: Tell me more.

John: It's hard to describe in worldly terms, as on earth we are so identified with the body. We have a hard time separating our awareness from the body. But in this state, here, now, there is no body, nor world in the sense as we know it. It is conscious awareness surrounded by an infinite reality in all directions.

P: Are you alone in this state

John: Again yes and no. Yes, in the sense that I am the light. I am that consciousness that is complete in itself. How can I explain? There is no past, no future, no activity, just being. It is full.

No, in the sense that there are many drops in the ocean. I am a drop, yet I am the ocean as well.

P: Yet you did come down, so to speak, to take up this body of John. Can you explain?

John: The body, the neurology, needs to become evolved enough so it can manifest the highest degree of consciousness. I don't have to die to experience this. It's as if the body is on one plane of existence and my true Self on another. The goal on earth is to experience this highest reality while in the body. So that there is no separation at all.

P: Is that possible?

John: Yes. Being in the body you are not of the body. Your consciousness is beyond the body.

P: That's what great saints like Ramakrishna, Ramana Maharshi and Yogananda have described.

John: It's the ultimate phase of human evolution. Until we reach that level we have to come back again and again.

P: Can you explain to me how you are able to experience this state now, while you are not capable of experiencing it when you are identified with your body during your normal day-to-day life?

John: That's why I came to see you today. I was led here. I've had glimpses of it during my meditations, but at the moment I'm having a hard time sustaining such states while in the body. Your facilitation is allowing me to let go of my bodily identification more easily. Today is just a reminder though. I have to learn to do this on my own.

P: Tell me more.

John: I'm in bliss right now. I feel like I am the light, I am consciousness, I am free. I want to stay here, or should I say, I want to experience this continuously. This is the true nature of who I am. I am not John. It's a role I play, like I have played roles so many times before in other bodies and at different times. It's incredible that this veil of forgetfulness comes upon me when I take up a body. I see things so clearly now. As John I doubt, I waver, I disconnect.

P: Why do you think this happens?

John: The mind and ego.

P: But where does it all begin? I mean, if you are by nature perfect already, where does this karmic journey through countless lives, start?

John: It's the play of Source Energy. It creates souls from within itself and reabsorbs them when awakened.

P: That's not really an answer.

John: Your question is only real from your standpoint. While embodied you feel the bondage so you will naturally wonder about how you got bound and how you can become free. But where I exist now, I am already free and the question is irrelevant.

P: What are you suggesting?

John: That the only way out is to experience the level of consciousness yourself. Here you're free. There is no birth or death here.

P: So you are suggesting rather than pondering the question as to where all of this started, I should change my level of awareness and the question goes away?

John: Yes, it's all about the state of your mind, or I should say your awareness.

P: That's what I tell my clients all the time. It's all in the mind. Your reality is determined by your state of mind.

John: But this state is even beyond the mind.

P: Help me understand.

John: The mind is an accumulation of impressions gathered during this and previous lives. It acts as a filter. You can't see reality in its purest form as long as you are looking through this filter.

P: So the mind is this filter?

John: The mind is wrapped around the soul. It's the astral body. The color of this astral body is your level of consciousness.

P: So if I understand this correctly, the soul doesn't have a color?

John: It's light itself, awareness itself, bliss itself. The mind is what is limiting the full expression of this light.

P: So in order to speak to me you have to some degree speak through the mind now?

John: Yes.

P. If I understand this correctly, the mind then is what causes one to be reborn?

John: The immature and unpurified mind. When the soul is ready it will drop it.

P: Can you tell me what is the nature of this mind?

John: The mind is the seat of the ego. It's the ego that separates.

P: Kindly elaborate.

John: The ego says 'I', which is not you.

P: Please go on.

John: It is only at this soul level we become one. We need to transcend all differences; ideas of race, sex so that we meet at the level of the soul. That's where we are all equal and one.

P: That's a task.

John: Collectively it is. Individually we can achieve it faster. Nobody can stop you from changing your awareness. Accordingly, your experience of reality changes.

P: True, as we change our minds and our state of consciousness, accordingly our world will change.

John: It will.

I get asked the question often: 'How is it that everybody seems to have a different kind of experience in the life-between-lives sphere? Isn't there just one kind of world?' It's a logical question. The problem with the question is the notion that the afterlife is a physical kind of place. A place that is merely an extension of this world as we know it.

What if there are higher levels of consciousness that take no particular form? What would 'communication' and interaction with such a frequency look like, and how would it be able to relate to us? Or, how would we relate, coming from all kinds of backgrounds, speaking different languages, born in different times and countries, from different upbringings, different levels of understanding? What 'language' would we speak? What kind of imagery would we use? Would one singular language do? What language would it be? Our language? We are conditioned by our parents, environment, and genes. We are unique in our own ways. We think according to the times we are raised in. Our understanding of things is based on this environment and culture and is uniquely ours. What if we would talk to somebody that was born five-hundred years ago, and we would try to explain to this person how we spend our days, how we travel, how we communicate and do our work? There wouldn't be much common ground to help us relate.

It's no different entering the afterlife. Communication with a higher intelligence is completely dependent on our level of consciousness. We carry with us the impressions from our past lives. These impressions, memories, if you like, stay with us wrapped around our soul like a sheath. The vibration of that sheath is our past. So when you look at reality around you it will always be like looking through that sheath. Even in the afterlife. So when a higher consciousness 'communicates' with us it will use the memories of our past to make us see things and help us understand. It breathes through us. It enlightens what is already there within us. It couldn't be any other way. We wouldn't be able to understand what lays beyond.

So nobody truly sees reality as it is. It depends on the degree of purity, or transparency, a soul has achieved while on earth. Purity, or transparency, while on earth, is a state where the subconscious impressions have been greatly reduced. The impressions of the past have been processed or even burned all together. It's a childlike, almost divine state of being. Where one man would look upon a woman with desire, another would see a manifestation of divine consciousness.

The latent subconscious impressions determine what

image you will see. It's like wearing dirty glasses. So while here on earth the task at hand is to clean the lens of our minds. Someone with a predominantly American mindset will translate his or her experience in the afterlife accordingly. A Chinese person according to Chinese traditions. He or she will see that reality in terms of American or Chinese concepts and symbols. It's what Carl Jung described as the conditioning resulting from the collective unconscious. He described the nature of the collective unconscious as a veil that is cast upon a group and that makes the group think about certain things in the same way. They think about religion, politics, money, culture in the same way because they have only been exposed to these things within the narrow boundaries of that group.

But if a soul has been able to shed the narrow confines of that kind of conditioning it will experience quite a different kind of reality. That is true both on earth as it is in the afterlife. Somebody whose veil of conditioning is completely purified would feel a complete unity with the ocean of consciousness in which it eternally exists.

Reality, as experienced by the enlightened ones, is very similar to the nature of reality in quantum physics. According to quantum physics, there is no object or location. The nature of reality, according to this science, is an infinite field of elementary energy. Similarly, to the enlightened one, reality is an infinite ocean of consciousness. The soul is a drop in that ocean. Subconscious debris, impurity, is what separates the individual consciousness from the consciousness of the ocean.

The nature of that infinite ocean, according to many spiritual traditions and saints who have realized it: is light, love and bliss. It is infinity. It is union. The true meaning of yoga is union. Union between the individual soul and this ocean of consciousness. The yoga as practiced today in many western yoga studios is an excellent preparation for the higher states of yoga. The physical interpretation of yoga helps the nervous system become calm and purified. But it needs to be taken to another level. The body is the temple of the soul. Through the different asanas and poses, we help the body and nervous system relax. This helps the mind relax. The next stage in yoga is to deal with the vibration in the mind. The waves of the mind need to calm down or even be eliminated altogether. The nature of these waves is the accumulated impression on the mind.

Everything we do, every action we perform or thought we have, leaves an impression on the mind. These actions either further purify or clear the mind or add other layers to it. So a higher interpretation or definition of yoga is that science that makes us aware of our actions, and alters these, in order to attain the purity required to achieve union with the true nature of reality.

This is the true nature of who we are. We are a soul. Our minds stand in the way of experiencing the bliss we could experience, if only we could get rid of the noise that is our minds. Deep inside, every soul longs for this peace and joy. Many people don't know where to look for that joy. They look for it in material and physical satisfaction.

Nothing in Western culture teaches us otherwise. But in many sensitive souls, after experiencing the shallowness of material pleasure, a longing arises for something higher, an internal peace that materialism can't provide.

Yoga is a science that can help people connect. It is not a religion. Anybody, irrespective of religious background, will eventually come to the same realization. It is an understanding of the nature of reality. What I mean by that is that yoga redirects our attention within. It reminds us that our true nature is divine. That we are a drop in the ocean of bliss and light. And that in order to experience that bliss and light within we need to quiet the mind. And that once that mind is sufficiently calm and purified it will be able to feel the nature of the ocean. That is union, the union of the soul with the peace, calm, love, light and oneness of the universe.

A pragmatist may wonder, how practical is all of this? But what is more practical than to live life in such a way that you always feel blissful, an inner peace, joyful and connected to nature and others around you? How practical is it to chase after material prosperity at the expense of peace of mind? It is more astonishing that so few ask themselves the question: why am I here on this earth?

I always ask my clients: how do you feel? You will always only be as happy as your state of mind allows you. Fortunate is that soul that understands this. Once you realize that the key to happiness is in your hands, your life will change. Realizing that the nature of your soul is divine, you will strive to manifest that divinity within. It is a simple concept. The source of joy we seek is within. Once the mind becomes clear and pure, the light that is already within can be experienced in the here and now. It becomes your nature. Imagine just for a moment you would experience such light and bliss. How would your life change? It would change everything. You wouldn't be so much concerned about career, money, prestige, reputation. You'd be happy regardless.

Once you are in the flow of things nature has a way of working in your favor. Much like what Gandhi said: Nature cannot supply your greed, but it will provide for your needs. The pursuit of material comfort will be subordinate to the pursuit of inner light and bliss. Each pursuit has its value, but the pursuit of inner happiness is paramount to a successful life.

To sum it up, the reason why everybody has a different life-in-between-lives experience depends on the mind of the individual. Or rather the veil. The impressions we gather in our lives are accumulated in the subconscious mind and when we die we carry these impressions with us. These stay wrapped around the soul. And the soul can only express itself to the degree the veil allows it. So one person with a particular kind of mental conditioning caused by its upbringing will consequently 'see' reality differently than someone else who may have done more soul work and carry less baggage, and who may see a much clearer image of reality.

The case of John allows us a glimpse of the nature of the soul. During all my years doing this kind of work and having seen hundreds of clients it is rare to come across a soul able to share this kind of knowledge. I normally get bits and pieces of information of this nature, but this case was very complete and clear. It allows us a perspective on our lives that is beyond the doctrines of established religious ideas. They don't seem to contradict our religious sentiments, but rather enlighten them, explain them and re-interpret them for this day and age.

Interesting too is the explanation of John that he is at a certain 'frequency' rather than in a place. From a scientific standpoint, this makes a lot of sense. What it seems to mean is that at our normal day-to-day cognitive level of conscious awareness our perception is limited. I can't see infrared or ultraviolet light, but that doesn't mean it's not here right now.

As the famous physicist Carl Sagan said: 'Absence of evidence is not evidence of absence'. To determine something to be true merely based on empirical evidence, that what I can see and observe, is severely restricting the possibility of that which may exist beyond what I can observe. The question I should ask myself instead is, how can I expand my range of observation. This, of course, is what science is trying to do, but it also means that what we consider to be scientifically true is merely that which science has been able to observe so far.

The spiritual regression techniques we use for past life regression and life-between-lives regression are designed to extend that range of observation. The reason I can't see ultraviolet is that ultraviolet light has shorter wavelengths than visible light. Although ultraviolet waves are invisible to the human eye, some insects, such as certain birds, bees and fish, can see them. This is similar to how dogs can hear the sound of a whistle just outside the hearing range of humans. But what if I could change my capacity to shorten my wavelength? Would this enable me to see ultraviolet light? Yes, it would. Similarly, when we apply regression techniques to the human mind it alters the wavelength of the mind. This can be measured and isn't rocket science. This makes the human mind capable of perceiving a reality that is outside the normal range of perception.

It's like listening to the radio. Let's say a large radio station simultaneously broadcasts several shows. One of these will be classic rock, another golden oldies, and yet another a live talk show. As I'm cruising on the freeway I tune into one of these channels, let's say the live talk show, and I become completely immersed in the lively discussion between the host and his guest. Everything else around me kind of disappears. The freeway, my worries, the weather, all seem to fade away and an hour later I suddenly find myself at my destination. During this drive, did the freeway cease to exist? Did the weather change? And, moreover, what happened to the other shows? Just because I picked this talk show doesn't mean the other shows stopped broadcasting. They existed, all simultaneously, but at different frequencies. By choosing the talk show I chose not to connect to the other frequencies.

When a client enters a higher state of consciousness,

another dimension opens up. Other shows that the universe is broadcasting become observable to the mind. In the new age world, the concept of the Akashic record is one such show. The Akashic records apparently are records of all human events, actions, thoughts, feelings and emotions, past, present and future, that are stored, and accessible on another plane of existence. It is eternally broadcasting and if my mind is high enough I can tap into that frequency and read these records.

It also explains how mediums are able to see what they see and do what they do. A good medium is able to perceive a range of frequencies that you and I are not sensitive enough to perceive. They tap into the range where souls dwell that have left the body behind. During a life-between-lives regression session, we tap into a similar frequency and we become capable of communicating with those that left our plane of existence. We even become capable of communicating with higher levels of existence. Quantum mechanics mentions eleven parallel universes. From the perspective of normal human consciousness, this can only be explained as universes that co-exist with ours, right here and right now, but that is not visible to us due to our limited range of perception. In the same way that evidence of quantum mechanics is mostly inferential by nature, the evidence for the veracity of life-between-lives regression is equally inferential. It is true to the observer. Somebody else may doubt your experience only because of failing to connect to the same frequency you just connected to. To you 'Absence of evidence is not evidence of absence'. It is real for you.

A great saint once told me on his death bed, 'Pieter, if you've really got something, you yourself will know. That's the criteria.' I love that and have tried to live by this principle: not to be too concerned about the opinion of others, what society thinks to be normal, true or acceptable and not to be too concerned about what science tells us to be true and not true. Instead, I trust my own discoveries and experiences. What I see, feel and experience within is my reality. Just because somebody else may not be able to see or feel this doesn't make it any less true or real to me. Do we need the approval of, or confirmation by others to feel how we feel?

Chapter 3
Seeking Integration

In order to fully understand the difference between a past life regression and a life-between-life regression, I'm dedicating this chapter to an almost complete record of a session where I guided a client through both the past life and the life-between-lives regression experience.

In this session, you will witness the power of a past life regression and what has been accomplished and experienced by the soul in a particular lifetime. What is also of particular interest in this session is seeing how we carry that learning into the life-between-life regression to further analyze and place it in perspective with one's current life tendencies and issues.

Jim is a successful publisher from Nevada. I noticed immediately when he walked into my office that he was an introverted and contemplative personality. Tall and strong, he had an air of natural authority. After we had a chat and I explained to him what to expect during the session, we gradually started the lengthy regression induction. During the early stages of the regression, I noticed he entered an altered state of consciousness quickly and deeply. When I regressed him further back in time we entered a past life:

> P: Can you describe to me your appearance? (*I generally ask many little questions but for the sake of the reader I have bundled some of these answers together*).
>
> Jim: I have long wavy brown hair. I'm wearing some kind of leather sandals........
>
> There's black hair on my toes and feet........ Brown pants, loose-fitting........ A white shirt that has buttons that are felt covered. Nothing fancy but it's a well-made quality material.
>
> P: Where are you now.
>
> Jim: In front of a house.... A log house amidst the trees.
>
> It's a slightly moist climate........ The house is set apart but not in isolation.
>
> There are others not too far away........ This is my house.

P: What else?

Jim: There is well with a garden plot here. It's France, or near France, central Europe.

P: What is your most significant observation?

Jim: It's a simple life. There is work to be done around the house and property. But not too much. There is time to be unaccounted for. It feels relaxed. I like it......... My name is Reynault.

There isn't anything too important to be done. I enjoy being here and the place where I live.

I'm progressing Reynault forward in time.

P: What is happening now?

Jim: I'm at a cobblestone town square. There's a fountain and buildings with different color facades lining the two sides of the square.........

There are people walking in different directions..........

It seems I'm in Brussels in the main square. I'm visiting..........

I've been here before.

P: Describe to me the outfits people are wearing.

Jim: Nothing extremely fancy, but well-made with some lace and frill and decorations. A few women with nice embroidered and gilded dresses. I see a few horse and carriages.

P: What date comes to mind?

Jim: 1745

P: What's your mood today?

Jim: I feel I there's something important for me here.

P: Move forward to that important thing you came here to do.

Jim: There's a big wooden door. Like the entrance to a church or an inner courtyard area. There's a slightly elevated platform above the street still attached to the square..........

There's a man, a religious figure with a robe. Dark red, flowing..........

Looking at me. Inviting me to come in through the door. I go in and walk down the cobblestone path. It brings me into a courtyard set apart from the square.

P: What happens next?

Jim: He's asking if I'm ready to join the clergy.

P: Is that why you came?

Jim: It is.

P: What do you answer, what do you do next?

Jim: I've hesitation. I can also feel that's why I'm here. I'm going to see it through.

P: Is it a monastic order? Which one comes to mind?

Jim: Something about a bishop. He's nearby. Catholic. A Catholic church. He's asking not to join to be a religious figure but to work for the bishop.

P: Are you joining to become a monastic or to be in

service to the bishop?

Jim: In service of the bishop. There's an invitation to join but it's not necessary to be part of the church itself.

P: What are you going to do?

Jim: He says the bishop has a job for me. That if I accept it there will be a blessing and payment.

P: How does this make you feel?

Jim: Feels like stepping into a new role. There is purpose. Something more than just living a life in a rural village.

P: Is that what you have been looking for, purpose?

Jim: Yes, it is alluring.

P: What's most significant about this moment?

Jim: It's a decision to work for something larger than myself. I say yes.

I'm progressing Reynault forward in time to another significant time in his life.

P: What is happening now?

Jim: I have armor on. It seems I have become a knight of some kind. Armor, a shield, white with a red cross. It seems I'm part of a crusade.

P: Are you in a group?

Jim: There are people around. We're moving on a march of some sort. There's many of us moving in the same direction. There's a caravan on a dirt road and we're all moving, walking, some on horse, a slow consistent pace.

P: What's the general mood within this group?

Jim: Determined.

P: What's your mood?

Jim: I feel like I'm part of something bigger than myself.

P: How long have you been walking and where are you going?

Jim: We're going to Rome. It's not going towards battle. It's coming away. The battle is over. We're the remaining battalion.

P: What's in Rome?

Jim: We're going to have an audience in the Vatican. We're going arrive in the square in front of the Vatican where we're going to hear a mass from the Pope.

P: How does this make you feel.

Jim: (*very emotional and crying*) Sad but also full of anticipation to be in the presence of the Pope.

P: What makes you sad?

Jim: Life has become more complicated. People got killed. But I'm alive and I'm having an audience with the Pope.

P: Go forward to the audience with the Pope.

Jim: (*very emotional*) I'm there, I kneel. He puts his hand on my head: (*weeping*) 'God bless you, child'. It feels divine, being recognized. I did something brave. I'm being given a command of some sort. Responsibility of overseeing a battalion. Almost a commission of being a leader in further aspects of the crusade (*still weeping*).

P: How does this make you feel?

Jim: Apprehensive but I'm committed. Such a beautiful surrounding.

P: Is that what is making you feel so emotional?

Jim: It feels like I have come so far (*sobbing*). From a rural village to kneeling in front of the Pope.

I'm again progressing Reynault forward in time to another significant time in his life.

P: Tell me what is happening now?

Jim: (*Very emotional*) I'm on a battlefield. The battle is over. I'm alive. There are many people dead……..
It's a victory.

P: Who's army are you fighting with?

Jim: French. But it's almost like for a Catholic order of some kind.

P: Like a papal army?

Jim: Yes, that's it. It's the church behind it. Not the French. There's a carriage. It's well decorated with white horses. Beautiful saddle. It's mine.

P: What kind of position are you in now, in terms of rank?

Jim: It's like commander (*even more emotional*). A commander position. A high rank.

P: What's your state of mind right now?

Jim: I'm indifferent to the death that has taken place. I feel like I've done my duty. Now it's time to go home.

P: You mean just going home, or leaving your command?

Jim: (*Ignoring the question*) I have a cape of some sort. Red velvet. With yellow lining. Like a prince of some sort. The carriage, the horses, it's though I am royalty of some kind.

P: Is that how you grew through the ranks?

Jim: It is because of the Pope and the commission. He was granting me some title. It wasn't a royal bloodline, but it was bestowed. And now I'm leaving the battlefield before going into the carriage and leaving the scene.

P: What's most significant about this moment, either around you or within you?

Jim: It's a wide expanse. It's the result of a conquest.

P: Who have you been fighting?

Jim: An Eastern European front. Somewhere past Hungary.

P: Is that how far you have traveled, all the way there for this battle?

Jim: I've retreated from the front and report back on the new territory that has been taken.

I'm again progressing Reynault forward in time to another significant time in his life.

P: Tell me what is happening now?

Jim: I'm inside of a church. It's me inside of a coffin. Is it? No, I'm paying respects. It's the Pope. I'm visiting the tomb (*weeping intensely*).

P: Are you sad?

Jim: I'm sad but I've mixed feelings. Remembering the opportunities he gave me. Paying tribute, respect.

P: What are the mixed feelings about?

Jim: It wasn't the life I expected that elevated me to a high station.

P: What do you mean by that?

Jim: I was never fully religious but saw the opportunity to be amongst powerful people that have access to more. To have power, to have responsibility. I feel sad the Pope is no longer alive. I feel as if I have done my duty and have excelled. I was given opportunities that others didn't have. I was chosen and that I have performed with impeccability (*again very emotional*).

P: How do you feel about that?

Jim: I feel that I have matured. It appears I'm now the king. I have this staff. I'm older. The robe is the same. It's red with a yellow outline. There is a crest on it.

P: How did you become the king?

Jim: It was part of the conquest. It came with the territory that I ruled.

P: Was that in the area of Hungary?

Jim: Yes, on the Eastern border. Prussia.

P: Did you change your name when you became king?

Jim: It's Richard.

P: What nation did you represent?

Jim: It's Prussia. It's a principality. I'm the king of part of the territory. It's part of an alliance of nations in that area.

P: How does it feel to be the king?

Jim: Now I'm older. Now I'm towards the end of my life as well. It feels like an accomplishment, destiny. It's not the desire for more any longer.

I'm progressing Reynault forward to the last day of his life as king Richard.

P: What is happening now? How old are you on this last day of your life?

Jim: Seventy-six.

P: Is there anything going on within you or around you that suggests your physical death will come this day?

Jim: I'm laying down. There's a number of people around. I'm somewhere within my territory. People are attending to me. There are people leaning over. Working on my chest and stomach. I'm coughing. Grey hair, weathered face. There are white sheets. People are sobbing.

P: What do you think about this life you just lived?

Jim: I'm grateful, feel that I accomplished a lot. And that the hesitation that I had when the offer was made evaporated into commitment and dedication to the task.

P: What did you learn?

Jim: I learned that power and responsibility are intertwined. In order to have power, one must be responsible for those he has power over. But that also there is a greater power above, and that even to be a king is not to be a God.

P: How do you feel you did?

Jim: I feel that I did well. I'm giving back a lot of land to the people and other principalities.

P: Did you feel you've been a noble king?

Jim: Yes, to the best of my ability.

I'm now progressing him to a place just after his death.

P: Where are you now in relation to the body you left behind?

Jim: I'm above it, looking down.

P: What are you feeling right now?

Jim: Separation. That the body is no longer who I am.

P: How do you feel about your death?

Jim: It was an easy passing. It wasn't traumatic. It was expected. It feels lighter.

As I guide him along, he describes how he moves on from here, slowly away from the place he died, to the higher levels of reality. He sees a group of five shapeless beings waiting for him there. He describes these as guides who welcome him to the other side. They take him through a corridor of light into a circle-like counsel room. A place of reflection where he can look back on his last life. He describes it as a projection on a wall of light where he can see multiple scenes of events that have happened during this last incarnation.

He expresses how light he feels without the burden of a body. He becomes aware of a presence much bigger. Much bigger and brighter than any shape could be. This energy is healing and recharging his energy. A nurturing, loving white light.

He then sees a vast expansive space where other beings sit in a semi-circle, telepathically communicating.

P: What's being said?

Jim: They are commending me on what happened in the past life and how it was largely in line with what we had determined before I entered it. The theme of nobility was accomplished. The theme of responsibility, power with responsibility, use of power. A humility, being dignified in the presence of whatever challenge.

P: Is there any constructive criticism that is being transmitted?

Jim: That I chose to pursue that calling to join in the crusade and the work within the Catholic Order at the expense of true love. I didn't have a love relationship. I had people that were under my command, people that were led to me, but love wasn't a main focus. It was a choice that I had.

P: So you chose power versus love, is that the gentle criticism you receive?

Jim: They said that I did it right, but that I didn't explore the theme of love. Love wasn't the hallmark of this lifetime. I chose to be a part of something bigger and being in a role of significance.

P: Now that we are here in the presence of the wise ones, is this is a good time to look at Jim's life and some of the issues relevant in his life? For example, if we look at the theme of Jim's life, and what the agreement was before he took his birth, and how this is unfolding so far, is he in line with this theme?

Jim: Yes, they say we can look at that. One of the wise ones steps forward and says that this last life as a king has parallels with the current life as Jim. The choice between pursuing a career calling, responsibility, attaining personal power and the opportunity for love.

P: Is it a continuation or a repetition of the theme? Is he repeating the same patterns again? Or is he aware of taking on this new theme?

Jim: It's an infusion of love in this dynamic.

P: So we're picking up from where we left?

Jim: Yes, it's a continuation in that sense. But he is aware this time.

P: How is he doing in that regard?

Jim: Right now not so good.

P: What can the wise ones recommend?

Jim: Embodying my spirit. Embody the power that I have. It's a natural evolution of my soul. Be more generous, more giving. That I can give love freely and it won't deplete.

P: Are you saying that he is holding back?

Jim: Yes, there is something of a disconnect. It's not fully realized, but it is birthing. It is changing now. It's at a juncture, a transition into more fully embodying the entirety of my soul and the spirit.

P: Are you saying he's birthing the integration right now?

Jim: Yes.

P: Is that the main theme of this current incarnation, to fuse these two elements? Or is there more?

Jim: There is a recognition of truth that appears to stand in sharp contrast with the experience of life and what's the structure of society; political and economic structures and institutions.

P: Yes, it's a far cry from the nobility when you lived your life as Richard isn't it?

Jim: It is lacking humility within the role of power and responsibility. It's sorely lacking.

P: What is Jim's task then regarding the integration of truth into his life? Is it more for him as an individual or does it needs to be expressed as a member of society? There could be more ways to express truth, right? Not everybody is a social being and truth can be realized as an internal experience. Where is Jim guided?

Jim: As a vessel, conduit, and also as being the prime mover. To step more out front on behalf of that truth.

P: (*Based on the issues he described on is intake form*) Is there a conflict in this regard?

Jim: I felt resistant, not ready to share the messages and ideas and the truth. I've previously in this life pursued things of personal interest and things that caught my attention, or seemed exciting. Truth has been in the background waiting for me to mature. I've been waiting to step into my own power with regards to it.

P: As a publisher?

Jim: That is a good vehicle to share and distribute information. But there's another piece that hasn't come alive yet, that I have prepared in terms of speaking, having an audience, a platform.

P: Trying to integrate love and truth into your previously accomplished use of power and responsibility, are there any obstacles standing in your way?

Jim: Just the distractions. The pursuing of surface level experiences of intimacy, recreational use of marijuana, alcohol. I'm moving beyond them now.

P: Are we maturing now then?

Jim: Yes, it is happening.

P: Since we are in the presence of the wise ones, what

could they offer in terms of advice or encouragement regarding the next step to take in this regard, perhaps in regards to the integration of truth, love, and power?

Jim: Let go of the fear. Let go of hesitation. Embrace the truth, embrace the theme, the reason that I'm here. And that what I perceive as problems now will begin to melt away. It's clearing out the old aspects of myself, to be cleaner. And to be in gratitude and maintain a sense of awe.

P: What are some of the karmas that you may have accumulated in this life that we may talk about? Or are these things worked out? What is the status of that, in relation to the integration we seek?

Jim: It seems I have worked through most of the karmas I have accumulated in this life, the bad decisions due to being out of integrity in relationships. During this change, people around me couldn't understand how I could change so much from being one way into a completely different person. It's at a tipping point now. Things could go either way. Either become more unpleasant and accumulate new karma, or it could go the other way and clear things up.

P: So it's kind of critical we are here today. How about we involve the wise ones and ask them what they can offer in terms of advice to make sure things tip the right way.

Jim: They say to be true to myself. Speak the truth. The whole truth. Put aside my reservations and fear of the outcome, and just continue to speak and be true to myself and to those intertwined with my life.

P: What is a good yardstick to use as a reference in regards to dealing with others, in the context of what you are trying to accomplish in this life?

Jim: They say I've done a pretty good job in letting go of those who I'm not in alignment with anymore, and that in order to attract and deal with others I need to make sure they will be in alignment with the values I cherish. I must be sure to have a proper understanding of peoples values, and only let those in that share these values. And that letting people in that don't share these values is the way to creating negative karmas.

P: So are we correct, in summary, that the values you describe are what we discovered today, the integration of power with personal responsibility, love, and truth? And that you need to use these values as your guiding principles? Have you been aware of this before today?

Jim: Yes, these are the values of my life. And no, I haven't been aware. Rather I sought out, as an experiment, people that had different values and lived in different ways to that what was internally congruent.

P: Are there any questions or issues that we may have missed? Either that you have or that the guides may want to share as final words of inspiration and guidance?

Jim: They say to stay the course. They say that I have all the pieces, all the capabilities. That everything has been set up to allow me to play out the themes and complete what I came into this body at this time to complete.

P: How do you feel about everything you have seen and experienced today?

Jim: I feel that I have a new perspective, a historical trajectory that led into my current life experience and I feel connected. That to see an opportunity and to act on it with integrity, humility and courage is the only path that is worth walking.

Chapter 4

The Ways Of
Higher Consciousness

It is a common notion that the life-between-lives or the afterlife is an extension of our life here on earth. In other words, we subconsciously project our ideas of life on the afterlife. We hope it is a world similar to ours, only without any of the negatives we encounter here on earth.

The problem with this kind of thinking is that we all have different ideas of life and death. We all like different things. People living in the desert may wish lush flowing rivers in their idea of heaven, whereas people living in flood areas imagine a heaven without any water at all.

For people more scientifically inclined these ideas can be quite off-putting. When they contact me to conduct a life-between-life regression, this is an important point to consider. One kind of scientific mind refuses to believe in any kind of afterlife world, though he or she is open to ideas of expanded consciousness and energy. Another group of educated people, in my experience, is not always conscious of their own logical and scientific approach towards life and death. Consciously, due to religious education and programming, they may carry romantic and literal ideas of heaven and the afterlife. But subconsciously they have been thoroughly educated to disbelieve religious doctrines in favor of scientific and rational thought. Though willing to experience a life-between-life regression and get in touch with something divine within themselves and beyond, they doubt they can do it or if it is possible at all. This can cause a conflict in their mind before and during the session.

When I started to conduct sessions in the early years, I dreaded extreme left brain intellectuals due to the simple fact that they didn't access the afterlife very easily. Some didn't access it at all. Though a small percentage, it nevertheless made me weary of working with them and trying to facilitate a connection to higher consciousness, however remote. Traditional life-between-lives regression is still very much based on a Christian-Judaic world and 'heaven' view. It still regards the afterlife as a well-organized, earth-like extension. There are guides, angels, higher beings, Akashic records, healing stations and so on.

The advantage I had, trying to solve this problem, was my extensive training in Eastern philosophy due to my many years as a student of Indian masters and scholars of the Vedas and Vedanta. My own education in Industrial Design also helped me be able to think logically and scientifically, so I could relate with the left-brainer. Further, my interest in quantum mechanics inspired me to create a bridge between traditional and scientific thought over to higher consciousness. And so I was trying to create a way where even the most extreme of my scientific clients would be able to connect to higher consciousness, without having to accept, consciously or unconsciously, a world-like heavenly sphere.

In order to share my solution and approach, I'd like to introduce some basic Eastern philosophical ideas. By eastern ideas, I mainly mean Buddhist and Vedic ideas. Since Buddhist philosophy, traditionally (though of course, it has evolved in myriad ways ever since), is mostly a spin-off of Vedic thought, I like to primarily focus on Advaitic (non-dual) Vedic thought.

The Vedic notion of the Soul is that it is already perfect. The Soul doesn't evolve. It is an already perfect part of a larger reality. This larger reality is regarded to be a formless ocean of consciousness. Its' qualities, if we may even qualify its' 'beyond-qualities' character, is called Sat-Chit-Ananda. This freely translates as – Existence, Knowledge, and Bliss Absolute. So the ultimate state, according to the

Vedas, is a formless and infinite ocean with the qualities of pure existence, infinite knowing and indescribable bliss.

What stands in our way of contacting this ocean of bliss is the multi-layered conditioning that has shaped around the soul, due to endless karmic entanglements and a lack of evolutionary awareness. It is not a lack of soul evolution as the soul never evolves. It is already as the nature of the ocean. But our awareness of our soul is trapped in a shell of karmic impressions and conditioning.

At the beginning of time, the ocean of consciousness has spit out, so to speak, parts of itself, and wrapped it in what we call evolution. Like a whirlpool spinning within an ocean, at no time is it ever not part of the ocean. The whirlpool is in the ocean, is made out of ocean water and pulls in and spits out ocean water. Similarly, the soul, though in the whirlpool of what we call evolution obscuring our ability to see it as soul, is always in the ocean and never exists separately from it.

This is very similar to quantum mechanics, where the idea of matter doesn't really exist. You and I see a multi-dimensional universe, even though this is not accurate at all. In reality, all that exists is energy. It is due to our sensory awareness that we perceive form. So we can say, scientifically, that the extreme limitation of our sense of perception is what causes us to 'see' diversity. In reality, there is no such thing as objects, even though we see them. And since there are no objects, how can we speak of these being located somewhere? There is no location, they are nowhere to be located in relation to each other because objects don't exist to begin with. All that exists is an ocean of infinite energy. The 'impurity' is our notion of separateness. I think I am, but I am not. If I am anything at all, it is a bunch of energy, vibrating at a certain frequency, held together by gravity and life energy, in an infinite ocean. Energy within energy.

Now, if we take this idea back to our world of regression we have a way forward. What if, with a certain group of people, we would ask them to simply tune into a different frequency. We wouldn't suggest that they go to either a past life or a life-between-life. We wouldn't suggest that such a place even exists. Rather, we would help them change their brain waves. They would intuitively understand that changing the brain frequency would allow them to perceive a reality corresponding to that frequency.

If a world of pure existence, pure knowing and pure bliss exists at a certain frequency we could learn to adjust our brainwave to such a state to get a glimpse of the existence, the knowledge, and bliss of what lies beyond.

This is not just theory. I have successfully applied this approach to many clients. During regressions, I switch them over to another frequency and I have seen incredibly beautiful states of mind unfolding.

I have different ways of slowly guiding clients into an altered state of consciousness depending on their individual nature and inclinations. The amazing result is that the client gradually loses identification with the body, and then with the conditioning of the mind, and actually enters an altered state of consciousness. He or she actually connects to a part of this quantum field, or oceanic consciousness, however you like to call it.

I believe that there are different levels and degrees or 'purity' of connection that depends on the subconscious of the client. The calmer the mind, the purer the connection.

Hypnotic regression is based on this principle. In our normal day-to-day cognitive awareness, (what is popularly called 'left-brain' awareness) the mind is in a Beta wave. This can easily be measured with biofeedback equipment. With even a bit of effort, we guide somebody into an Alpha state (a more inward or 'right-brain' inner awareness). By continuing to use advanced regression techniques, we help one enter a profoundly deep Theta state. This is a super heightened state of awareness, similar to deep meditation.

An expert meditator can access this state independently. But most people need a bit of help. Facilitation can help us step away from the endless chatter of the Beta state into quick and easy access into the Theta state. The problem an inexperienced meditator has is that, with a mind stuck in left-brain Beta consciousness, he or she is trying to orchestrate access to a right-brain Theta consciousness. The left brain is trying not to be in the left brain while applying left-brain methods. The facilitator can take over the role of the left brain and apply the methods on behalf of the client, who then can let go more easily, thus allowing easier access within.

Once the client has tuned into the Theta state of consciousness we can start to discuss issues relevant to the person's life. The person, once connected, will experience an incredible sense of detached clarity about him or herself. In this state of transpersonal, trans-conditioned perspective, the client will be his or her own therapist.

More often than not, in this state, I witness an incredible sense of peace and joy in the client. It has made me a believer that indeed the nature of this quantum ocean is existence, knowledge, and bliss. For many of my clients, this is their experience of life and is not mere theory anymore. This is significant.

Almost anybody can access higher states of consciousness. It is part of who we are. When we go to sleep at night, you might be surprised to learn what states our mind travels through: From Beta to Alpha, through Theta into Delta*. Normally you wouldn't be able to consciously enter and linger into the Theta state. But with the facilitation of an experienced and qualified therapist, you can. During a regression we are capable of holding your mind in a prolonged Theta frequency, allowing you to access regions of your deep subconscious, and, importantly, allowing you to touch the quantum ocean of a higher consciousness that stretches infinitely in all directions, beyond the mind. Here you can touch existence itself, knowledge absolute and infinite bliss.

EEG Brain Frequency Chart

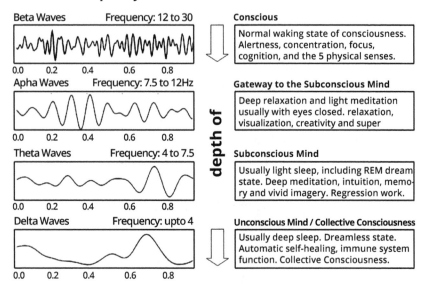

Beta Waves   Frequency: 12 to 30

0.0   0.2   0.4   0.6   0.8

Conscious

Normal waking state of consciousness. Alertness, concentration, focus, cognition, and the 5 physical senses.

Apha Waves   Frequency: 7.5 to 12Hz

0.0   0.2   0.4   0.6   0.8

Gateway to the Subconscious Mind

Deep relaxation and light meditation usually with eyes closed. relaxation, visualization, creativity and super

Theta Waves   Frequency: 4 to 7.5

0.0   0.2   0.4   0.6   0.8

Subconscious Mind

Usually light sleep, including REM dream state. Deep meditation, intuition, memory and vivid imagery. Regression work.

Delta Waves   Frequency: upto 4

0.0   0.2   0.4   0.6   0.8

Unconscious Mind / Collective Consciousness

Usually deep sleep. Dreamless state. Automatic self-healing, immune system function. Collective Consciousness.

depth of

*Beta (12-30Hz): Beta brain waves are associated with normal waking consciousness and a heightened state of alertness, logic and critical reasoning. As you go about your daily activities you are in Beta. Although important for effectively functioning in everyday life, higher Beta levels translate into stress, anxiety, and restlessness. With the majority of adults primarily operating at Beta during their waking hours, it is little wonder that stress is today's most common health problem. The voice of Beta is the little nagging chatterbox of your inner critic, which becomes louder and more relentless the higher you go in the range.

Alpha (7.5-12Hz): Alpha brain waves are present in deep relaxation with the eyes usually closed and while daydreaming. The relaxed detached awareness achieved during light meditation is characteristic of Alpha and is optimal for programming your mind for success. Alpha heightens your imagination, visualization, memory, learning, and concentration. It lies at the base of your conscious awareness and is the gateway to your subconscious mind. The voice of Alpha is your intuition, which becomes clearer and more profound the closer you get to 7.5Hz.

Theta (4-7.5Hz): Theta brain waves are present during deep meditation and light sleep, including the REM dream state. Theta is the realm of your subconscious mind. It is also known as the twilight state as it is normally only momentarily experienced as you drift off to sleep (from Alpha) and arise from deep sleep (from Delta). A sense of deep spiritual connection and oneness with the Universe can be experienced at Theta. Vivid visualizations, great inspiration, profound creativity, exceptional insight as well as your mind's most deep-seated programs are all at Theta. The voice of Theta is silence.

Delta (0.5-4Hz): The Delta frequency is the slowest and is present in deep, dreamless sleep and in very deep, transcendental meditation where awareness is completely detached. Delta is the realm of your unconscious mind. It is the gateway to the Universal mind and the collective unconscious whereby information received is otherwise unavailable at the conscious level. Delta is associated with deep healing and regeneration, underlining the importance of deep sleep to the healing process.

Gamma (30-100Hz): The most recently discovered range is Gamma which is the fastest in frequency at above 40Hz (some researchers do not distinguish Beta from Gamma waves). Although little is known about this state of mind, initial research shows Gamma waves are associated with bursts of insight and high-level information processing.

An important footnote to this chapter is the realization that no matter what regression method one uses, the experience of each client is true in its own way. Each experience shows different aspects of a world that lies beyond our normal perception. I'm not advocating that one perspective of that reality is superior or truer than another. Rather, the experiences of my clients are the result of their different inclinations. Neuro-linguistic programming (NLP) has a beautiful way of explaining this; "nobody actually sees reality as it is. We only see our map of it."

To the degree that our mind is completely devoid of any conditioning, is the degree to which our experience of the afterlife becomes clearer.

This reminds me of a conversation I had with a great Indian saint near Paris, France. He had appeared to me in a dream and bestowed upon me a sacred mantra. Excitedly I asked him: 'Are you my guru now?' To which he answered: "You are your own guru. If I say I am your guru you will, because of your love for me, always do what I teach you, repeat the mantra I give you, even when you get older. But you will change. You will evolve. And with it, your idea of God will change. What you need to progress further will change too."

This has always stayed with me. We do change and so do our needs. Accordingly, our perception of the world around us changes. As our mind changes, so will our reality. We can never say with absolute certainty that this is true and that is untrue. The Indian philosopher Vivekananda gives a beautiful example: Let's say you make a picture of the sun from your back yard. Now let's make a picture of the sun from a place just beyond the atmosphere. Now let's make another one from within deep space. When you compare the three images they all show the sun. But each will give you a completely different image. The sun never changes. But our perspective of it causes us to see different things. Yet, each picture is equally true. You can't say that the image taken from your backyard isn't accurate or a bad representation of the sun. It is the sun and it's accurate. The image of the sun taken from deep space is equally true and accurate. Yet it allows us a more detailed view.

What my clients experience during a regression is just like this. Each person equally witnesses an image of the afterlife. Yet each person is looking at it from a different perspective. Some from the backyard, some from just beyond the atmosphere and some from within deep space. And each experience is equally valid and equally true.

Chapter 4: The ways of higher consciousness

Chapter 5

Awakening

This past-life story begins with a 24-year-old dark skinned barefoot man dressed in rags. His name is Bahri. He recounts living in a rugged area surrounded by large high peaked mountains. His tribe is here with him and they live in primitive white skin tents. He expresses a need to help lead this tribe somewhere else due to a lack of food. He's in Europe in a barren hot place, long ago, before civilization as we know it, started.

I move him forward to when he is 53 years of age where

he shares with me how he is now tired and getting older. It's dry and he is thirsty. People come to him for advice and he guides the tribe where to go and what to do. He's now a tribal elder. He loves the fact that he is finally able to be of service. He used to be a master archer and is now teaching the youngsters. They eat mostly big game and berries. He's peaceful and content. There are no worries. He can just be.

Moving forward in time again he is now much older and sick. He's inside the tent. People around him are staring at him and sobbing. He's dying. He's aware he's dying and on reflecting back on his life he describes a contented life. He learned to help others and is happy with this.

I now guide the soul to the life-between-life state. In her current life, Karin is a 22-year-old Law student from Las Vegas.

You may wonder how we 'choose' the particular past-life we return back to during the session. The reality is that we don't choose consciously. The suggestion during the session is 'go back to the most relevant past life'. Looking back on all the past-life and life-between-life regression sessions I have conducted, I feel that there is a higher consciousness that guides us through the process. Considering that most of us have lived countless past lives, that we don't remember, it definitely wouldn't be a conscious choice by the client. As a therapist, I obviously don't know the past lives of my clients either. My conclusion is that it is either the higher consciousness of the client or a guiding principle that makes this choice for us during the session. This becomes particularly obvious when you consider that the issues brought forward during the life-between-life part of the session almost always ties in perfectly to the patterns we discover in the past-life regression. It is quite amazing how this always seems to be spot-on. A higher intelligence seems to integrate this learning in a way we consciously can't easily achieve.

She describes following a few bright lights that guide her through a tunnel. She's expressing great happiness and excitement. Upon exiting this tunnel, she finds herself for a while in a quieter, darker place when a blue light form approaches her. This light slowly takes the shape of an angel. His name is Gabriel. He tells her to calm down as she feels intimidated and overwhelmed. She follows Gabriel to a group of other angelic beings.

P: Have you known them before?

Karin: Yes, I was part of them.

P: Are they like a Soul Group or more like protectors?

Karin: More like angels and I'm part of them. I'm much happier and calmer now. So excited to be talking about things with them.

P: What is it you'll be talking about to them? Do you sometimes talk about the life you have just lived, like an overview?

Karin: Not now. That comes later. We're just catching up. It's not even talking. It's just feeling.

P: How do you experience that?

Karin: It's hard to describe. Kind of entangled energy together. Like a big gathering. It's like a harmony, like someone striking a few cords on a piano.

P: What is your color like?

Karin: Like a yellowish purple.

P: Where do you generally go to discuss the life of Karin (*her current life*)?

Karin: I need to talk to Gabriel. He doesn't seem too forthcoming. He just seems to look at me very intensely. It's a happy energy. He just tells me to calm down and not to second guess myself. Somebody else steps forward.

P: How does this presence present itself?

Karin: He's like Gabriel but has a different purpose. He'll answer my questions.

P: How does the conversation transpire?

Karin: He says I'm on the right path. I wanted to help people as best as I could. I'm very intuitive and brought over a lot of knowledge. I just need to listen to myself. I want to care for other people.

P: In what way would the wise ones suggest you help others in this life as Karin?

Karin: I have the ability to inspire other people. I need to help them see how they can help themselves, so they become motivated by themselves. It seems I need to speak.

P: Any particular topic or direction?

Karin: I see that it's the Law (*she's a Law student now*). I have a lot of experience apparently. In other lives. It resonates.

P: What did you do in other lives?

Karin: Stockbroker. I owned multiple businesses. Big and small businesses.

P: Would these businesses and Law career be by themselves a way to help others or provide you with the means to help others?

Karin: Both. They're intertwined.

P: You earlier wrote down a question regarding your observation that you tend to feel emotions much more deeply than others and that you wonder why this is? What can you tell me about this?

Karin: Experience.

P: Interesting. I think I understand what you're trying to say but kindly elaborate.

Karin: I've had a lot of different emotions in different languages (*lives*), and I understand them naturally.

P: Is anything specific standing out?

Karin: I hear love. It's love.

P: Is anything standing in the way?

Karin: It's a lack of discipline. I need to meditate and connect more.

P: I hear this a lot. What does this discipline in regards to meditation mean in practical terms?

Karin: Because I feel and relate to so many different

emotions, I understand almost every side, argument and situation. I find myself feeling certain opposite ways about the same topic. I need to meditate to come to a middle place.

P: Are you implying that the meditation would allow you to find and maintain a spiritual center?

Karin: Yes, that's it.

P: You mentioned earlier to me (*in her intake form*) confidence.

The intake form or questionnaire is a critical part of the session. Clients write down what it is they would like to ask when they meet a Higher Source. During the session, at an opportune moment, I ask the questions on behalf of the client.

Karin: I'm feeling self-confidence in a sense of self-power because I'm connected a lot of the time. But sometimes I over-inflate myself because I think I'm just Karin here, but I'm actually sensing more than that. I shouldn't attribute it to what I am just here.

P: Are you saying that when you feel that power you think it is coming from Karin but that in reality, it is coming from a higher Self? And that Karin should be more aware of that?

Karin: Yes. I need to better differentiate that the source of all power comes from the divine. I'm awakening. Maturing.

P: What does this mean, awakening? What does the guide say?

Karin: The ultimate direction where I want to go with this awakening is to help others get freedom. Both material and spiritual freedom.

P: Is that how you see your awakening?

Karin: Freedom. Yes. It's a state of consciousness.

P: How do you see this unfold in your day-to-day life? What's the vision?

Karin: This is coming from a past life. I was a spiritual leader that brought me great self-worth and I would empower other people. I brought that with me.

P: Tell me more.

Karin: I was in Athens. I was some kind of priestess. I just know this.

P: Was this a one-time occurrence?

Karin: No many times, it has been a theme.

P: Did you already attain awakening in those lifetimes or is this something you're growing towards just in this lifetime?

Karin: No I already attained it.

P: In this lifetime, as a 22-year-old, did you already catch up with this awakening or does it still needs unfolding?

Karin: I'm hearing 'still baking'.

P: Is there anything else we may need to pay attention to or what we may have missed?

Karin: They say that I should pay attention to dreams.

P: I see, kindly elaborate.

Karin: Through dreams and through meditation, they can remain in contact with me, the guides.

P: How does this make you feel?

Karin: I feel very wise and fortunate.

I often hear other regression therapists say that you cannot have a successful regression with young people, as they haven't gathered enough life experience yet. My question as a regression therapist is, 'which life'? I've had amazing sessions with young people. Not only is their mind often purer and simpler and much more capable of connecting to a higher frequency, but often we underestimate the fact or forget that they may have lived many lives before. The term 'old soul' is very applicable to the soul in this session. A young body doesn't mean a young soul, nor does an old body automatically makes for an old and wise soul.

There is a lot of confusion amongst people when they see powerful and shrewd people in places of power and authority. They wonder, how come that this guy can rise to such height but with such a lack of integrity? How come that I, when I feel myself to be so sensitive and intelligent, am not recognized or in an elevated position? There are several ways we can answer this question. The first is the mistaken assumption that intelligence and wisdom are one and the same thing. In my opinion, intelligence is hereditary. It's the brain you step into when you take up a particular body. It is neither a sign of spiritual advancement nor of great wisdom. A soul may want to live in a body with a brilliant mind for a while because it can offer particular growth and learning opportunities that it needs in this phase of its evolution. When we look around us and even look at some of the leaders of our country, we cannot deny their intelligence and cleverness. It takes a certain kind of intelligence to rise to the top. We simultaneously see in many of them a complete lack of integrity, altruism, and wisdom. These characteristics manifest only when a soul is evolved. Such a soul may not be interested in power, and even if such a soul could wield power, like our king in chapter three, he would use it wisely and for the greater good of others.

A wiser soul, generally, has gone beyond the need for recognition and power. Its main interests are spiritual by nature. It wants to love, help, learn, teach and share. The kind of intelligence of a wise soul is different. It's the kind of intelligence that has discernment between what is going to lead it to greater inner freedom, and what is going to further tie it down to the world and endless future rebirths. It is a superior kind of intelligence that is not dependent upon absolute brainpower. Its source is inner purity, clarity. It is derived from the purity that has taken place over many lifetimes, where layers of conditioning have been removed from the soul, allowing the higher Self to shine through unobstructed. In ancient Sanskrit text, they call such a mind Medha or Buddhi, the enlightened consciousness.

A clever and intelligent mind can be, from a spiritual perspective, a double-edged sword. Yes, it can help someone be very successful. But at what expense? If this intelligence is not accompanied with wisdom it can lead the soul astray. It can bind itself with so many karmic burdens that it can take many lifetimes to unwind this bondage. It may reap the benefits of its intelligence for a while until karma holds it accountable. Not in a punitive way, but as a tool to help this soul become aware that every action has a reaction, equal and opposite. A soul may have to go through these experiences in order to wake up.

I've met many greatly advanced spiritual souls who did not have any particular worldly achievement nor were they interested in them. It's not that they wouldn't have been able to achieve greatness even in a worldly sense as some may well have been very capable. Some of them, on the other hand, were very simple-hearted and other-worldly and may not have been known for their great intellectual prowess. Yet in their presence, I detected a great awareness and alertness, as if they could see right through you. I remember, as a part of a powerful religious Order in India, that some of its leaders were not the most spiritually advanced. Often, though not always, it was the simple brother who was most enlightened. It is a rare privilege if you meet a highly advanced soul that has both head and heart.

It is important to note that a great intellect is not a requirement or indication of spiritual awakening. Love and awareness are.

Karin went back to the beginnings of time, even before

civilization began, where she could re-experience the origins of her altruistic tendencies. Journeying through many lives she attained inner awakening and used this power and love to be of service to others. Though in this body and at a young age she has not yet fully manifested the earlier attained inner awakening, she can already start to feel this inner power waking up. The innocent and matter of fact way in which she shares her struggles to contain her power and confidence are charming. It's also a clear indication of the deep memories and tendencies of past lifetimes and the re-awakening of her earlier spiritual achievements. She knows how to use her brain and intelligence in the best way. Not over-emphasizing her career or intelligence, she emphasized service and love instead.

She has come to the realization that all power comes from the divine. And she starts to feel in her life that this power is starting to manifest. She's learning not to get carried away by this intelligence and power, but to become more aware that it is coming from a higher place. In a previous birth, she already attained a high degree of spiritual awakening and currently, in her life as Karin she is preparing herself to manifest this awakening once again. She is coming to understand that her true identity is not Karin, but a divine free soul that is beyond Karin

This is a highly significant realization. Many spiritual traditions describe the goal of life to be the awakening of the Self. Karin is starting to understand what this means. What is the experience like for somebody who is awakened? It is easier to understand when we look at it through the lens of life-between-lives regression. Because such a soul, while being firmly grounded here on this planet, would know its true identity to be something or somewhere else. It wouldn't regard its true identity to be the body or even mind. It would know and feel at all times that its true identity is the higher Self, the Soul. It would know and feel that it is ever free and never changing no matter what body it may take up for a while. It would at all times remain aware of and be connected with the divine source consciousness. It's like living in two worlds at the same time. The ups and downs of the world wouldn't affect such a soul much. It would have a way of rising above things.

And this is the reason why experiencing a life-between-lives regression can be such a powerful journey. Imagine, that even for a moment, you get to feel for yourself that you are more than just this body, living in this town, surrounded by this culture and these people, stuck in this job. That instead you are an ever-free divine light being. Imagine that you truly feel and understand, not intellectually but experientially, that the journey to this plane of existence is a mere training program, and is temporary. What psychological implications would this have for you?

A lot of our pain and suffering originates from feeling stuck, not seeing a way out or forward. We freeze or panic. All we can see at that moment are the narrow confines of our existence here on earth. We can't see beyond it.

We don't have perspective. All the conditioning that this incarnation placed upon us; parental, environmental and genetic condition, has become real to us. We have become a human body, forgetting our eternal light identity.

The goal of spirituality is to reclaim the awareness of our true Self. We may struggle to catch a glimpse of this super consciousness state from our own spiritual practices. Yet with the help of a facilitator during a regression session, it becomes so much easier to experience this for yourself. The relief it gives to the mind can be tremendous. The relief it gives to the mind can be tremendous knowing and realizing that there is a way through because I am so much more than I think I am in my day-to-day life. Knowing that I have lived many lives before means that I need not be so afraid of and intimidated by the circumstances. This can be cathartic.

I can share with you from my own experiences that during the hardest times of my life I found such strength knowing that this life is just a temporary dream. Not only because of the work I do and witnessing hundreds of clients' experience higher consciousness but from my own spiritual experiences as well. It started, as I shared with you before, by remembering several of my past lives. It made me wonder at an early age, why am I here and what is my true purpose. I didn't find much satisfaction in pursuing what most people seem to blindly pursue. I was looking, early on, for an experience that would reconnect me with my true identity, beyond the limited confinement of this body and world I felt trapped in now. This search put me in contact with several mystics who would help me rediscover this truth.

One such encounter was in Amsterdam with an Indian guru. This sage had taken up temporary residence, at the invitation of some sincere seekers, in a house on the outskirts of Amsterdam. I felt an immediate connection with him and wanted to be near him and visit him as often as I could. Living near Paris at the time, I would take the train and go see him every chance I got. During one such visit, he invited me to meditate with him in his little homemade shrine. This was a small room he had converted to a little sanctuary, with some sacred images, incense, candles, and meditation cushions. The higher frequency of the room was palpable. I had been practicing meditation for a while and every so often experienced deep inner peace and calm. This preparation helped me when in his presence, to quickly reconnect with this calm and enter into a deep meditation. After a few minutes of peaceful silence, I suddenly felt I was leaving my body, then my mind. The bliss that ensued was beyond comprehension and cannot be expressed in words. I experienced that I was a light consciousness expanding infinitely in all directions. There was still a thin veil of self-identity remaining, but only to the extent that it allowed me to witness the bliss and expansiveness of my own being. The next level would have been for me to completely dissolve into this infinity around me and within me. A state, I learned later, that one most probably wouldn't return from.

I don't know how long I stayed in this state. It was much later when I felt myself pulled back into the body and reconnecting with this plane of existence. As I slowly opened my eyes I saw the sage looking at me compassionately and he said: 'hmmm, not bad.' He had witnessed the whole thing. To this day I still don't know if he facilitated this experience for me or that it was the osmosis of his presence that allowed me to have this incredible experience. What I do know is that it changed my life.

During my own life-between-lives experience I experienced a similar state of consciousness. A state where I was simultaneously aware that my body was in the room with the therapist, but my higher Self was beyond this world.

These experiences have confirmed for me the power and reality of the transcendental experience. When a client touches that frequency I'm able to some extent travel there with them. I find a smile on my lips every time encountering these wonderful and pure beings. My greatest joy is when they rediscover once again how beautiful and great they truly are. We are all children of light.

Chapter 6
Living Free

There is an important difference between a regular therapy session and a life-between-lives regression session. During a regular therapy session, the therapist tries to understand, over time, what issues are troubling the client. This may be a lengthy process and even then, it is often hard to make a proper diagnosis and work with the client to overcome these issues. I have never met most people before conducting a life-between-lives session. Yet people come to these sessions with a list of personal and important issues they need to know more about. As a matter of fact, I ask them to write down, before we meet, what they would like to know about themselves and the purpose of their lives.

As a life-between-lives regression therapist, I don't really need to know what best way is for you to move forward. How could I ever know your life's purpose? Of course, a good psycho-therapist will try to help you find your own answers and can be instrumental in helping you achieve this. But these things take time, and you still don't really know how much of it is right for you because solutions are being sought within the boundaries of your current understanding. Perhaps, and most likely, the solution lies outside your current belief system and understanding.

A life-between-life regression session is based on the notion that there is a world beyond our current world, and that this world is occupied not only by departed souls but by ascended guides and masters. Some of these masters have lived on this earth before, and others haven't. During the session, I have discovered, these beings assist us in our quest for answers. We are being guided. I even believe that no client visits my office randomly. Everything is arranged from above, whether we are aware of it or not. I consider it my sacred duty, therefore, to regard each client as a case specially assigned to me by the guides and masters. So I do everything I can during a session to find what we set out to discover.

The idea that we are guided becomes especially obvious when we start the past life regression process. During the regression, a sacred power helps the client choose the life that is most relevant for our session. It guides the higher Self of the client to pick the life that has helpful information needed to unravel important issues.

Often, when we enter the life-between-life world, a guide appears that the client can talk to and get answers from. Sometimes a client is guided to the Council, a board of wise beings who can shed light on the client's progress so far, and who may offer further guidance and advise on how to proceed from here onwards.

It is not uncommon for the client to start speaking in the third person about his or her own life offering advice and counsel when the client steps into a higher state of consciousness.

This advice is more powerful than any therapist could ever offer. It is presented from outside the sheath of conditioning that is wrapped around each person's true identity. This advice is trans-personal, or as I sometimes call it, epi-conditioning; outside of our conditioning, not colored by the previous impressions of the client. It is offered outside the conditioning and the limits of this current life.

Philosophy is always built on some basic premises, certain foundational principles upon which we build our reasoning. No matter how coherent we try to be, at some point we make a choice as to what seems most logical to us and build our case from there. In this case, we assume that we are a soul and that we reincarnate governed by the law of karma. Guides and ascended masters complement these fundamental principles.

In order to have a better session, I spend at least 20 to 30 minutes talking to a client just before we start the actual regression. This is not only designed to make the client relax, get comfortable and to build rapport, but it serves a larger and more important purpose. With this 'pre-induction' talk I help the client eliminate basic misunderstandings, overcome subconscious fears and remove blocks that may otherwise show up during the session. This is a critical part of the session and is as important as the regression itself.

One of the issues I address during this talk is the idea of unfiltered communication. To express yourself freely in a higher state of consciousness is not as easy as it may sound. We're not used to it. It is rare to be prepared to share our feelings and express the true nature of our inner being.

Ever since we were kids we might have been told to keep quiet. When we expressed our true feelings we might have been told to either shut up, get in line, adjust to others or do what is expected of us. Perhaps we could freely share our feelings with our mom or dad, but we quickly learned we couldn't do this at school, around friends, and in society at large.

Imagine you are at work in a meeting, surrounded by high ranking officials and executives. And the CEO asks you: "I would really like to know what you think about this issue. Please share with us your intuitive observations and your feelings as a soul. We greatly value what you feel and sense and I'm convinced it will enlighten us."

Does this ever happen? Unlikely. And even if somebody would ask your opinion it would most probably be quickly overridden and you are offered advice instead.

So we have learned to 'adapt'. We filter what we say, and eventually, after years of conditioning, we even filter what we think. We only say those things that we consider safe. This is mostly an unconscious process. But what about our true feelings? What about our instincts? What about our intuition, that quiet inner voice? After years of repression, these have become more subdued than you realize.

This conditioned self-expression shows up during the regression session unless you are made aware of this issue beforehand. When you are let loose in a state beyond these environmental and parental conditions it may take you a minute to give yourself permission to express yourself freely. You are simply not used to it and your first instinct, even here, will be to filter and censor what you say. Your first tendency will be to only tell me what you think I want to hear or what you think is proper.

But this isn't about your therapist, who is just a matchmaker between you and the superconscious reality. This is all about you and everything about you is important. What you feel, sense and intuit. As a matter of fact, I'm trying to find your real voice. I'm trying to have you experience and express that side of you that is not affected by the conditions of your current life. So that you remember once again who you truly are and what you came to accomplish on earth this time. This is just one of many lives and when, even for a moment, you realize this you'll find the courage to step away from the old layers of conditioning that prevent you from being your true authentic Self.

Some people are so conditioned that they have become afraid to speak freely. I help them find that voice. There is nothing more beautiful seeing someone in a higher state of consciousness break free and start to express. It's as if the floodgates open up. When this happens and they hear themselves talk, they often have a sense of disbelief for the simple reason that they don't trust themselves yet. But after a while, as they continue letting go, it all starts to make sense.

There is a tremendous sense of liberation when you allow yourself to flow, be and express freely. A regression session lifts you out of your limited day-to-day consciousness into a free-flowing expression of yourself. A consciousness that is drenched in worldly conditioning will completely limit you from remembering who you really are and who you have always been.

Behind this dense mind fog, your true and ancient Self is shining.

When you learn to connect, you start to become a conduit of the divine. It is much more logical than you realize. When in normal Beta consciousness, in other words, when you are your normal day-to-day self, you have stepped into the role of your current personality. Like you step onto a theatre stage and play your part. As long as you are on stage you act out your part and you can't really think about much else without messing up the performance. Similarly, it is hard to be connected to a superconscious state as long as you are attached to this world. You have to get off stage and drop the character you're playing to remember who you are.

The task at hand is to find a way to quiet down the noise of your life to listen and connect to the parallel universe of your higher consciousness. It is here already. It is always present. But you are tuned into a different frequency. At first, you may have to physically leave the stage to find a quiet place to connect. But with practice, you can develop the skill to be always connected. It is at that point that you become a divine conduit. This can manifest itself in different ways according to your temperament and the skills you have developed over many lifetimes. You may become a teacher, healer or even a prophet. Even if you would hold a normal job, or hang out with friends and family, these divine qualities would manifest and influence your environment.

I find evidence of this tremendous inner potential during the life-between-lives sessions. It never ceases to amaze me when just an hour earlier a client walks into my office and seems to be leading an ordinary life, to moments later share with me tremendous spiritual insights in a superconscious state. The question we may ask ourselves is: how come I am able to experience these phenomena when in a superconscious state, and not during the day when I am at work or at home?

The first obvious reason is the mind frequency you are

in at that moment. But this brings up another question. How come I can't be connected to a higher frequency all the time? Or, more accurately, how come I am never at his frequency? I don't really know if I can answer this question. Because in order to do so I'd have to answer the question; "Why are we in this world to begin with and how did it all start?" I'd have to understand why this world evolved and continues to unfold the way it did.

I could provide you with lofty philosophical theories and answers, something I love to do, but it would still not truly answer the question as to why I am in ordinary consciousness now. What we do know is that it is possible to attain a higher state of consciousness and experience a superconscious state of enlightenment. So rather than wondering where this all started, it may be more helpful to find out how we can attain and maintain a superconscious connection. It reminds me of a short anecdote I read, about a man who entered a mango orchard and started to count the number of mango trees, then the number of leaves and mangoes, noted everything down and started writing a thesis about orchards. While he was busily engaged, a simple and pure-hearted farmer walked by, plucked a mango and started enjoying it as he sat down in the cooling shade of a big mango tree.

At some point, I may want to break the cycle of my never-ending busy and inquisitive state of mind and enter a more blissful state of being. Like the farmer craving a juicy mango on a hot summer day, I may be craving inner peace and an enlightened state of mind. Sure, I am interested in the grand philosophical questions, but I'm needier of that fruit of divine bliss and tranquility. Philosophy is only second to actual experience and although it's very important as a guiding principle, there comes a point in our lives when we may want to taste the mango.

Real spirituality is an inner experience. It's not theory, not even believing or having faith, but an inner knowing based on an actual personal inner experience. There is a difference between somebody who has studied the map of Paris, knows every alley, even the street names and places of interest, and somebody who has visited Paris, felt its special ambiance and has absorbed its long history from the vibrations of the old city walls and cathedrals. No amount of study of Paris maps, nor having faith in it, can ever give you a true understanding of the inner spirit of Paris. You have to go and experience it for yourself.

So we need to experience the bliss of a higher consciousness ourselves in order to truly understand it. It's kind of an ambiguous topic. Most people don't even know there is such a thing as a higher state of consciousness, and even if they do, they don't see what it can do for them. Why strive for something or build a life around a phenomenon when you don't see what possible good it can do? Accordingly, most of us emphasize a comfortable life in the world and subordinate or even ignore, the attainment of a superconscious state to that. But for those who have actually experienced this state, they know how tremendously blissful it is and how wonderfully intelligent, infinite, free and aware you feel. Once you touch that reality you start to disregard the importance of worldly life and start to subordinate it to the attainment of this state of bliss so that you can experience it all the time.

And this brings me back to my earlier question, how can we maintain such a state all the time? It begins by building a balanced life. We will discuss in a later chapter how the three pillars of life; love, spirituality, and safety are the foundation of the attainment of a superconscious state. These pillars are the cement blocks upon which we will build our superstructure. It is critically important, because even if you get a glimpse of a superconscious state, and you haven't prepared this foundation, you wouldn't be able to process it properly to maintain and hold a balanced state of mind.

What happens next once you built your balanced life? In my experience we have to practice certain spiritual disciplines in order to progress more rapidly than the natural course of evolution will take us. Especially in our Western culture, this is a new concept. We are familiar with body culture, with working out to stay fit and healthy. We're even familiar with mind culture, with studying and achieving academic success. But we're unfamiliar with applying this discipline to our inner and spiritual life. For that, we have to look to the Orient. When you look at some aspects of Buddhism and Hindu Vedic practices, for example, you get a much clearer idea of how these groups have developed a spiritual culture with specific practices designed to attain a superconscious state.

I'm not at all suggesting that we have to become Buddhists

or Hindus. I'm just pointing to some cultural and spiritual elements in these places from which we can derive some inspiration. I think it is better to stay within our own cultural identity, rather than wasting valuable energy, the energy we need to progress, adapting to other cultures. I myself made that mistake. I spent so much energy adapting to Indian culture when I lived there for over a decade, that I would have done better using that energy dedicated to the practices I learned there and applying it within my own cultural setting. It would have saved my health and I would have advanced more quickly.

We need to learn and acquire spiritual knowledge. There isn't much knowledge here in our Western world when it comes to spiritual advancement. And with this, I mean in terms of actual practices other than prayer and having faith. The emergence of yoga schools everywhere is a great development, but by and large, most of these schools still emphasize body culture over inner culture.

Again and again, we hear from the ascended masters, during a life-between-lives regression session, that we have to meditate. Meditate, meditate, meditate, is the message. Few of us really know how to meditate. Meditation is a highly individualized practice. You can't point to one specific practice that is superior to another. Even if we meditate at all, we like to meditate in different ways. It has to do with cultural differences, temperamental differences, and philosophical differences. Let me break this down. When I say cultural differences I mean the setting and our cultural identity. For example, a person may be predominantly Christian and likes to meditate surrounded by Christian symbology, like pictures and statues of Jesus and Mary. Another person may feel more comfortable meditating in a personal shrine filled with Hindu deities like Hanuman or the Divine Mother.

Temperamental differences point to differences in the way you like to meditate. Some people like to meditate while they connect to nature, like sitting on a rock in the forest or taking a long walk along a river. Whereas others like a more intimate and quiet place where they can shut the doors and be by themselves.

By philosophical differences, I mean the way you think about your God and your end goal. The nature of your meditation depends on what you hope to attain and what you want to connect with. A Christian may want to see and be with Jesus in a heavenly sphere, whereas a Buddhist or Vedic inspired philosopher may prefer meditating on an infinite ocean of consciousness.

And on top of that, as we progress, our idea of God and the nature of reality changes and evolves. It is a never-ending unfoldment. As layers of conditioning get taken away from us we start to perceive different things and understand reality in a new light.

This leads us to the most important realization. Through meditation and spiritual practices like breathing exercises, we purify and calm our mind. As our mind becomes calmer it helps us get closer to the superconscious reality. So no matter how we meditate, the immediate goal is to clean the subconscious and conscious mind of old impressions and conditioning. This will translate to an immediate change in the perception of our world.

Perception is everything.

The masks of our conditioning are what prevents us from seeing and connecting with our highest truth. It's our own beliefs and habits that stand in our way. Being able to lift ourselves above this world into a transcendental state of being, we learn to become free. A life-between-life session can help us with this, and it often directs us to become more pro-active in our meditation. Once we understand this, then practice, we can come to a state of being that is always connected to the highest reality. We first connect to what lies apparently beyond, then bring it down to our world. It only appears beyond when we have not yet learned to connect. But once we do connect, it isn't 'beyond' anymore. It is experienced in the here and now. In India they call this Jivan Mukta; 'one who is inwardly free while living in this world'.

Section 2

The Pillars Of A Balanced Life

This second section describes the three pillars of a purposeful life; love, safety, and spirituality. We learn that the purpose of earthly life is intimately connected with our soul's purpose and divine nature. Once we become aware of the true nature of our Being, this realization has natural consequences for how we start living our life now.

This section shares accounts of those who have become aware of different aspects of the 3 pillars of purpose, and how this awareness impacts the remainder of their lives. We discover that there are two levels of purpose, an earthly one and a divine one. And that the earthly purpose only becomes clear once we understand our divine purpose. It is only by understanding the divine nature of our Selves, that can we start to make sense of what we are here to do in this lifetime and how to achieve it.

Chapter 7

Living The Enlightened Life

You may wonder whether, after conducting many life-between-lives regressions, I may have observed consistent themes that seem to repeat themselves during these sessions. The answer to that question is a simple yes. I divide these themes into two main categories. The first category is instructions from the guides, or from the higher Self of the client. These serve to remind the client to be more aware of the impermanent nature of this world and to be more focused on making a connection to that higher reality in order not to get too stuck to this temporal existence. Most of the chapters in section one of this book highlight this theme.

The second category is specific instructions on how to live a successful life here on earth. Success here is not only measured by the first category, i.e. making a connection with the higher Self, but also by living a life in the here and now that is truly enlightened. Of these life instructions, I have identified three main sub-themes that recur, either shown separately or sometimes together. These are love, safety, and spirituality.

Below I've drawn a triangle with a theme in each corner. Each theme forms a pillar or cornerstone of life. The idea behind this triangle is that not only is each pillar important by itself but that the synergy between the three pillars is what makes for an enlightened life. The sum becomes more than the parts.

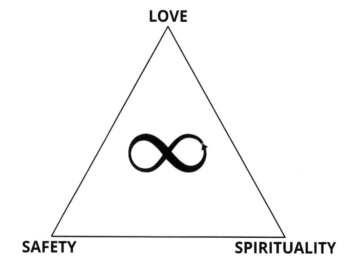

Let me elaborate on each pillar by itself, and then look at each pillar in relationship to the others to understand how this relates to living an enlightened life.

LOVE

We all want and need love. It's a prominent theme when clients come to see me for a life-between-life session. Reconnecting with a loved one after a loss, looking for a soul mate, trying to understand the complex karmic entanglements between souls, these are all love themes that deeply engage us. It seems quite obvious that love is one of the pillars of a happy life. Not only cultivating a loving disposition but primarily trying to intimately connect with another soul is what we all seem to be looking for. In the life-between-lives world, when we are not connected to a body and worldly circumstances, the soul yearns to reconnect with a soul mate, a soul group, a guide or a higher consciousness. Whatever it is we may long to connect with, it is always a loving energy of some kind.

Perhaps, in our quest for meaningful connections on earth, we have a deep-seated unconscious memory of our undiluted and pure love connections of the in-between-life state and seek to experience that here. The problem that we face here on earth is that the embodied state stands in the way of experiencing these higher forms of divine love. It is hard to just love because we have to pay taxes, pay the rent or mortgage, deal with other people and infinitely changing circumstances. These circumstances take us away from our center and pull us in a million different directions, often in ways that are anything but loving. Trying to just love while ignoring the world around us is a noble and lofty concept, but very difficult to achieve. We are intimately connected with people and circumstances around us, and unless we have a clear vision of how we relate and fit into the grand scheme of things, we will struggle to maintain a composed and loving disposition. The world around us tends to pull us away from our attempt to love.

Let me give you an example. Let's say you are young and deeply in love. You feel blessed to have met the partner of your life. Life seems beautiful and you feel like you can conquer the world. It is all sunshine and roses. For a while, things seem to be going great between you and your loved one, until one day you really long to live together. Up to that point, you had nobody to look after and you slept in your parent's basement, or on your friend's couch. You didn't need to work too much and your needs were few. But now that you have a partner and you both need a roof over your head the needs increase. You need more money. Things need to change. Your lifestyle needs to change. You need to work longer hours and come home tired. You can't spend as much happy time together, unconcerned with the world as you were when you were dating. Reality has kicked in. Your lack of resources becomes a constant source of stress not only within you but between you and your partner. It seems to limit your plans for the future. You had wanted to travel together, hang out together, sit on the beach together, but all you do now is work. Your need for financial security and safety has compromised your love.

So even love, the sweetest and strongest of love gets compromised by a need for financial security and safety. We need to feel safe and secure and we need money. When we feel safe and secure it becomes much easier to express love more freely.

SAFETY

Yes, it is obvious that in order to feel safe and secure we need money. Everybody seems to strive for it. Yet, few people have a healthy relationship with money. In order to feel safe and secure, money has become a goal unto itself. We even measure success in terms of money. We think that the more money we have, the more successful we'll be As a matter of fact, we dedicate so much of our daily energy to the pursuit of money that we hardly have a life left. As a great man I know said: "We spend our lives preparing our bed, but nobody gets to sleep in it." We are spending a disproportionate amount of time and energy working. The question is why?

We have forgotten our true purpose. Living a comfortable material life seems to have become our purpose. Not just comfort, we seem to want an ever-increasing level of comfort. It is not enough to just have a comfortable home, a car that can take us from point A to B, but we need a luxurious mansion and the nicest car. We are not aware that all of this comes at a premium. More work. Longer hours. More time away from our loved ones.

We set up a life so we could be together, hang out together, be in each other's loving company, and now, in order to sustain that ideal, we need to work. Longer and harder.

There are plenty of people that have succeeded in making a lot of money. The reasoning has been, well, let me work hard now so I can have the time to live later. Only to find themselves, at the end of their career, completely alienated from their loved ones. What they had to do in order to make the money was counterproductive to maintaining a loving inner disposition. Is that what we call successful?

Others that have neglected to strive for financial independence are paying a heavy price too, worrying and anxious, eroding loving relationships in the process, not having the time or ability to pursue things of higher interest.

Is there a middle path? How do we deal with our need for safety and security in the context of love and spirituality, amidst obligations, commitments, and family? To come to a middle path, we need to establish a vision of what our life could look like if we strengthened each pillar. Money is only useful to the extent that it allows us to spend time with our loved ones or when we have time and energy left over to create a personal and family situation in tune with our greatest spiritual aspirations. When you are safe and have attained a level of comfort and security, striving for more security won't add anything to your life. Sometimes an unhealthy internal relationship develops between the meaning of feeling secure versus a need to make more money. What once was supposed to make us feel safe and secure, i.e. money has now become a goal in itself. Not for the attainment for security (because we are already secure) but now for the sake of wanting more entertainment and enjoyment. The moment you make money a goal or a requirement in itself, out of context with the other two pillars of life, you lose sight of the great purpose you're trying to create for yourself and your family. What is important is to re-evaluate what we really need individually or within the context of our relationships. A great example is a rising interest in tiny houses. Young families are refusing to take on a 30-year mortgage. They would rather work less and spend more time with their family or traveling valuing freedom over comfort. They have to sacrifice living in a larger house but in return, they enjoy a life unencumbered by financial pressure and endless work. You are just as secure and safe in a tiny house as you are in a 4000 feet mansion. Perhaps even more secure because you don't have an expensive mortgage that is controlled by a bank that doesn't really care about you. Wanting that big house is not anymore a question of satisfying the basic need for safety and security, it is now a desire for more enjoyment, prestige, and comfort. The question to ask ourselves is how does this sacrifice, this price to be paid, bring me closer to my vision? Is it adding to my internal peace and balance or taking away from it? Looking at the relationship between the three pillars and how much time and energy we spend on each individual pillar at the expense of the other can help us make that determination. . Real success is finding that perfect balance.

SPIRITUALITY

The third pillar is spirituality. Connecting to the spirit within us and the spiritual consciousness around and beyond us. Again and again, during the life-between-lives sessions, we hear from the guiding consciousness that we need to remember who we truly are. That we are not this body or this person we think we are now. We have lived many lives before. This is just one more. We are reminded to become awakened to the fact that even while we are on this earth it is possible to remember, to become aware of our divine identity.

This has huge implications. If you think about it, with this kind of awareness, we learn to wake up to the realization that this earth isn't our only home. We learn to step away from fear. The root cause of fear is the reptilian survival mechanism trying to survive on this planet. It is a deep-rooted instinct that we as humans have inherited through thousands of years of trying to survive in a hostile environment. But it pertains to the human body. Constant material striving is an extension of this primal fear to survive. It's instinctual. Yet unenlightened. Because what constitutes survival? How much is enough?

From a pure survival standpoint there comes a point where we don't really need more. Once the basic human needs are met we are safe enough. Having two cars or five houses doesn't make us more secure. It doesn't contribute to an increased level of safety.

There needs to be a balance between the amount of time

and energy we dedicate to the pursuit of wealth. It needs to be in proportion to the amount of time and energy we dedicate to our loved ones and our inner life. Any excess in either one direction or the other will take away the energy that is required to maintain the other aspects, thus compromising the balance that is required to live an enlightened life.

There is an interesting concept about happiness which proposes that there are different levels of happiness. The first step is to depart from the old paradigm that more is better. Changing this paradigm allows us to be open to looking at different ways and levels of happiness. By understanding these levels, we can systematically elevate our consciousness from the mundane to the divine. The higher we rise on the scale of happiness, the better will we be able to maintain the balance between the three pillars of life.

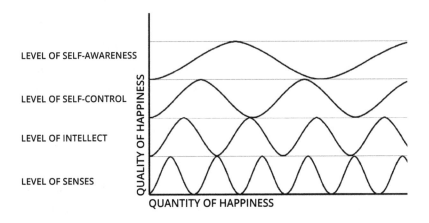

This concept proposes two different aspects of happiness. In this image, the x-axis indicates the quantity of happiness. The y-axis is the quality of happiness. A movement along the horizontal line simply means I simply accumulate more and there is a quantitive increase in happiness. But that doesn't necessarily mean that I will have a higher qualitative experience of life. The paradigm flaw is to think that if I have more of something that I will become happier.

I can take one piece of chocolate and the innate quality of the chocolate will only give me a certain amount of enjoyment, a certain amount of happiness. If I eat two pieces of chocolate, I don't increase the quality of happiness. I create a duplication of a certain level of happiness. In this case, eating one piece of chocolate produces a short wave. Eating another piece of chocolate creates a second wave. If I take ten pieces of chocolate, I have ten waves. The innate quality is not improving. That explains why a billionaire still wants more. He buys one yacht that is ten feet, then upgrades to buy a 50' yacht, then a 100' yacht and still remains unsatisfied. He is not increasing the quality of happiness. He accumulates and consumes, yet is unaware about the possibility of an increase of awareness, which is basically rising along the y-axis, to increase the quality of happiness.

Why are we witnessing an increasing amount of people interested in things like yoga, meditation, and mindfulness? Perhaps we are becoming more aware of the fact that though we may have everything we seemingly need, we're still not happy. When we accumulate we are merely increasing the quantity of happiness. We're not increasing the quality.

Things like music, art, and reading are of an intellectual nature that elevate the mind. When you're reading a good book, watching a good movie or you're a pianist playing a beautiful sonata, the mind is able to stay in a happy place much longer than when you eat a piece of chocolate. If you eat a piece of chocolate the satisfaction lasts just five seconds. Any sensual experience, however exciting, lasts only a short while. You can see in the diagram that the wave of sense enjoyment is very short whereas the wave of intellectual enjoyment is much longer.

It's a higher as well as longer wave. Somebody who is more intellectually enlightened is on a higher evolutionary plane than somebody who is merely indulging in the senses. The people who can't rise above the senses focus on sensual and sexual gratification, procreation and food. That's all they care about. They are not capable or interested in conceiving that there's more to life.

The man of intellect also has a relatively larger capacity for sorrow. As his mind rises higher it can also come down deeper. The relative ups and downs are much higher for the man of sophistication than for the sense-oriented people. The sensual soul only goes up and down within the range of the senses as the wave on the diagram indicates. The intellectual can go up and down much higher. It is ironic that as we become more enlightened, the relative rise and fall of the mind also becomes more pronounced.

The level of self-control is higher in the intellectually enlightened individual because this is a stage of development where, to a certain extent, the senses are under control. We're not driven by sensual impulses. We have intellectual capabilities to understand abstract concepts and the consequences of our actions. At this level, there is an understanding that if senses are allowed to run riot, nothing will ever be achieved.

Self-control is an interesting concept. When we obtain a natural level of self-control the waves of the mind naturally start to subside. We become calm. Self-control doesn't mean suppression or denying the senses.

It means we can handle our senses. It doesn't mean we should be abstinent or live like a monk. On the contrary, it means that we're able to do things in a balanced, natural way. We learn to listen to our body. We only eat when we're hungry. We make love when we want to, but are not compelled. We're not at the mercy of our senses. The sensual ones are at the mercy of their senses. Self-control is where one can use and step into the senses but are not controlled by them.

When you gain natural self-control, without the need for repression or being ruled by the senses, you're becoming balanced. A certain peace starts to unfold. As you can see in the diagram, this level is characterized by a much longer wave. The wave is also high on the scale of qualitative happiness because the mind is naturally calmer.

Something deep within starts to unfold. It is as if a power

that is inside of us starts to manifest. Peace is not coming from outside. A mind that is under control is always a calmer mind. Those that are in control of themselves are calm, collected, rational and emotionally balanced. This balance allows for a manifestation of inner light, an inner power.

At this level, there's a certain joy that starts to happen within the self-controlled person that's coming from within. Sense enjoyment always requires an object of gratification, whether it's a piece of chocolate or another person that you want to enjoy. Intellectual enjoyment also needs constant engagement with something intellectual. Somebody who's self-controlled will start to find peace coming from within that doesn't need an external source. When you are at peace and balanced you have fewer desires. There is a level of self-control where you go through moments feeling just quiet, without needs or desires. You just feel good. It requires balance not to be compelled and forced into perpetual motion because of the draw of the senses or the pull of the intellect.

At this level of self-awareness, the mind is moving into a very high state of consciousness. Looking at the diagram we see that self-awareness is characterized by a very high and long wave. People that are self-aware are on the verge of complete awakening. Everything in their life is under control and balanced. If you look around, you will notice that the people that are more awake are more careful. People who have natural self-control are aware of what they eat, medications they use, and the company they keep. They are aware of the environment, other people and exhibit empathy and kindness. Complete Self-awakening, a fifth level, could be a level even above self-awareness. This level wouldn't even be characterized by waves, but would just be a flat horizontal line. Complete equanimity of being, a state beyond mind.

In order to move up in awareness, all the lower levels need to be brought under control. There needs to be self-control over the senses as well as the unfolding of intellectual capacity. As a result of mastery of these first two levels, one now starts to become very self-aware. The self-aware person is by default a happier person. An unhappy mind is a mind dragged down by uncontrolled habits. Most of our problems are caused by this lack of self-control. Problems with drinking, smoking, drugs, bad moods, medication or diet are accompanied by unhappiness. Those who are self-aware and whose life is fully under control will be happier because the waves of their mind are very gentle and they experience higher consciousness.

In the present moment, someone who is aware and more awakened is charged with an incredible amount of knowledge, love, connection, and understanding. The awakened person is happier and lives with an expanded range of emotions, understanding, and state of mind. The awakened one experiences a different reality than one who is not awake.

Imagine what happens when I call you on my cell phone. My phone is set to a certain frequency as I dial your number which is then sent to the cell tower to be sent on to you. When you answer, you open yourself up to my signal as I also open myself up to yours. My frequency is being sent to the tower which influences in a small way the frequencies around me. By communicating with you I open myself to your signal.

Similarly, every thought that is sent out into this world around us affects this world. It's like a radio frequency. If I am broadcasting my thoughts at a certain frequency, just like radio waves, everyone else at that frequency can receive my transmissions.

When your mind is at a certain frequency and the world sends out a similar frequency, your mind receives that frequency.

My subconscious mind is that transmitter of frequencies and based on the conditioning and state of my mind, I transmit a specific mind frequency. We know now that ninety-three percent of all communication is non-verbal. We may not be aware that our body language, the intonation of our voice, and the energy being projected outward is affecting the world around us. But people pick up on these frequency signals. We gravitate towards people who have the same frequency signal that we are transmitting. If it takes two signals that are mutually attuned to get information, and I want to listen to a specific radio station, I need to tune into the exact frequency being sent out. Similarly, I will attract all the people, the things and opportunities that resonate with my frequency.

This is why certain people always attract bad company

and that's why others always seem lucky. That's why certain people find love or become wealthy and others don't. Their subconscious mind is like a cell phone. The tremendous secret is that what you emit and transmit is also sent back to you, like the tower communicating to you through the frequency you have opened up to. We help people in our practice to re-attune their subconscious mind to whatever it is they want.

This is a phenomenal concept because if bad things are happening to us and negative energy is coming our way, we have to realize this is because of the negative frequency that is sent out with the mind.

Nothing comes to you that you are not attuned to. A radio station that broadcasts at a different frequency than what you are tuned into cannot play on your radio. You will not hear the show unless you tune into the accurate frequency. These incoming and outgoing forces are naturally attuned. It is a scientific concept that what I get back from the world around me is the same frequency that I am sending out.

Lao Tzu reminds us, therefore, "Watch your thoughts for they become words. Watch your words for they become actions. Watch your actions for they become habits. Watch your habits for they become character. Watch your character for it becomes your destiny." This is the wisdom of the ages.

John Tettemer, in his book 'I was a monk' gives a beautiful description of the experience of awakening consciousness:

"Let us imagine that one of the cells of my body was suddenly awakened out of its ordinary, little consciousness, concerned with the functions and activities of its existence, and was carried up into the larger consciousness of myself. It would be bewildered by the otherness of this larger life: it would know that what were unbelievable mysteries in its smaller life had a perfectly natural explanation when seen from this wider perspective; it would smile at all the systems it had built up to explain its life and the world about it, as being hopelessly naïve and founded on its very limited experience.

When it returned to its ordinary state of consciousness, it would not express itself in terms it had attained during its flight to a higher realm, but would know forevermore that there was a larger life into which its smaller existence fitted, and that only in terms of that life could its individual life be understood. It would never again attempt to explain reality in terms of itself. It would bring back with it a conception of a great unity in all the apparent confusion and separation of its earlier experience. Strangest feeling of all, it would begin to realize that the most fundamental conception of its little consciousness – which made it say to itself: "I am, I live, I act" – was an error, caused by the consciousness of the activities taking place within its organism. Through its flight it had lost this sense of 'I', and now realized it for what it was – a fiction, a figment, created by its own mind as the cause and doer of all that happened within it. It knew now that there was no separate 'I', but that that larger life lived in it and through it. I would recognize this sense of 'I' as the source of all its personal unhappiness because it had sought to live in terms of itself and not in terms of that larger life from which, as a center, all things were happening. It would perhaps conceive of this other life momentarily experienced as its God, and would feel that the height of wisdom would be to surrender this erroneous conception of 'I' and say: "Not my will, but Thine, be done." If it still dared to trust itself to cast its experience in a formula, as was its old custom, it must say: "God is, I am not." Or in moments of exalted feeling, it might cry out: "I live, yet not I, but God, liveth in me."

To conclude this chapter, when we look at safety, love, and spirituality as a synergetic force that, when balanced, is key to living an enlightened life, we have a recipe for happiness. By investigating which of these pillars are out of balance, with some being over-emphasized while others are being under-stimulated we begin to become aware of what kind of frequency we broadcast.

We may spend too much energy on the accumulation of wealth, at the expense of love and inner peace. We may still be under the illusion that more is better. Or maybe we have love and feel safe and secure, but in spite of this still, feel a sense of dissatisfaction. Perhaps we have not been aware that there are different levels of happiness and that it is time to attune ourselves to the higher aspects of life and Self. We may have been under the illusion that once love and safety have been achieved we would automatically be happy, only to find out this is not true.

Whenever we feel out of sorts, as if there is something not

quite right with our lives, all we need to do is look at the three pillars of life. These will show us what aspect of our life needs work. Invariably one or more of these pillars are under or over stimulated.

It is very rare to find somebody who has achieved a perfect balance between the three pillars. Such a soul is truly free, inside and out. In such an enlightened soul you find a perfect balance between a life in the world that is free and independent and a high state of consciousness that is connected to the highest frequencies of this universe and beyond. Such a soul is able to both completely embrace life as well as transcend it.

There is a beautiful saying: 'the bee came to suck the honey but became stuck to the honey pot.' The art is to be able to enjoy and embrace life, but it requires a perfect inner balance and greatly developed sense of self-awareness not to get devoured by it. When we learn to equally strengthen the three pillars of safety, love and spiritual awareness we can sip the honey, without getting stuck to the world, and be able to keep our minds attuned to the highest aspirations of our soul. That is a life well lived. That is true success.

Chapter 8

The Higher Purpose Of Grief And Loss

This chapter is about the pillar of love, and how a loss of love threw this person out of balance. It's about her attempt to find herself again and to regain her internal state of love and balance. This is an account of a 54-year old Registered Nurse Emily, who came all the way from Indiana to see me in my office in Asheville NC. In her pre-session questionnaire, she described her struggle with the loss of her husband, grief, and trying to make sense of it all. She wrote:

'I scheduled a life-between-lives experience to help me find and define myself. I feel restless and that I am walking in circles...... The urge to find out more became demanding after the death of my husband 8 ½ years ago. What started as a journey to find him has turned into a journey to find myself. It has been a journey that has taught me a lot about myself but has left me with more questions than answers, and the need to answer them. At this point in my life I'm not sure what it is I'm supposed to be doing. I just know I have this restless need to find something, which leads me to believe I am not fulfilling my purpose at this point.'

This chapter will highlight how a journey back through time to a previous birth, and a subsequent life-between-life regression journey, helped her to better understand why this loss happened to her. It also offered a much greater insight into how she could take this loss and move forward in a new direction, something that up to this point in her life seemed unimaginable. Particularly inspiring is the help she received during the life-between-life session from her guide and a counsel of highly enlightened beings that stepped forward offering her insight and advise.

Loss is something that we all sooner or later will have to experience. There are multiple aspects to the loss of a loved one that makes it so challenging. Not only is there the actual loss but there is also much more going on, the 'why' questions. Why is this happening, why now, why in this way, what does it all mean? The reality we face that is often overlooked after a loved one passes on is that their support and help dealing with life has been taken away. As this same client wrote to me:

> 'I realized after I lost my husband, that not only was I missing him, but those weaknesses in myself that he propped up. When you lose someone, not only do you face their loss but your own weaknesses that you relied upon another to overcome, you now have to face both.'

It is my hope that sharing this case may not only bring a greater sense of understanding but also a degree of relief, knowing that a higher power and greater good is there with us, looking out for us and helping us grow.

The story starts with Emily traveling back to a time in Europe, around 1750, where she described herself as a young woman in service of a wealthy family. She was a happy person who was content with her life, happy to be of and in service. After she described that interesting though uneventful phase of her life, I progressed her forward in time to a relevant event.

P: What is happening now?

Emily: I see her sitting in a room.

Interestingly, throughout this past life regression, she describes the events of her past in the third person, as a witness. This isn't completely uncommon, but most people 'enter' the experience. As a regression therapist, when encountering a traumatic event, I may use this 'stepping above it' approach as a way to have a more detached look at the experiences in question. It is generally not something the client him or herself initiates, but something the therapist may encourage. She continues the descriptions of her life in a very matter of fact and detached way.

> Emily: At a desk. Grey hair, salt, and pepper. It's a fold-out desk. She's in a bedroom, her bedroom.

Tentatively I'm testing to see if I can get her to 'step into' the experience as herself, but she continues to describe the events in the third person.

> P: What are you doing here in your bedroom?
>
> Emily: She's writing.
>
> P: What is she writing?
>
> Emily: She seems sad. There's been a loss.
>
> P: Can you tell me about that?
>
> Emily: I'm not sure who it is.
>
> P: Is this setting familiar? Whose house is this?
>
> Emily: It's hers. I think she lost a spouse.
>
> P: How old is she?
>
> Emily: 50.
>
> P: Do you have any children?

Emily: Some girls.

P: Are they nearby?

Emily: They are near, in town.

P: If you intuit the gist of what she is writing, what can you tell me about that?

Emily: She's resolving a business.

It is normal during the past life regression (and not necessarily in the life-between-life regression, where souls are freer and often more chatty) that the client answers in terse and short sentences. The client is deeply engrossed in the experience and is also taking on the characteristics of that person living at that time. I've seen, though it may be a bit of a generalization, that people of a bygone era were not as outspoken as we are today. A slow and soft voice is also characteristic and indicative of somebody absorbed in a deep theta state.

P: What kind of business?

Emily: Her husband's.

P: She has to look after these affairs now?

Emily: Yes.

P: What is she doing during her day-to-day life?

Emily: She's just existing.

P: Help me understand, what does that mean?

Emily: She's dissolved the business. A shipping business.

P: That was her husband's shipping business?

Emily: Yes.

P: How is she doing financially?

Emily: Fine.

P: So there is no more need to work in service I assume?

Emily: No.

P: Why is she dissolving the business?

Emily: She can't run it on her own. It's per his instructions.

P: How does she feel about that?

Emily: It's her duty?

P: Ok. So tell me, where is her house right now?

Emily: It's on the street. Cobblestones, houses made of stone.

P: What country comes to mind?

Emily: France.

P: Where in France, with what kind of climate?

Emily: The South, it's warm.

P: How has her life been ever since she was in service? Give me a general overview?

Emily: Comfortable, a lot of friends. A lot of purpose.

P: In what way, purpose?

Emily: Societal.

P: Help me understand, what does that mean?

Emily: Her husband was well off. So she stayed busy

in the town. Helping other women.

P: In what way?

Emily: Helping poor families? She was kind.

P: What is her name?

Emily: Catherine.

P: What is most relevant so far?

Emily: It's been a joyful life. Not hard, comfortable.

P: How does she feel about her husband's passing?

Emily: Resigned.

When I progress her forward in time, she describes how she's in bed with a chronic and terminal illness. This then makes me move her forward to the last day of her life as Catherine.

P: What is happening now, on this last day of this life as Catherine?

Emily: She's in bed. She's ill.

P: What's her age now?

Emily: 59.

P: Is there anything going on within her or around her to suggest that her physical death will come this day?

Emily: She's surrounded by her girls.

P: How does the body feel?

Emily: Heavy.

P: How is the mind?

Emily: Peaceful.

P: How do you feel about the life you lived as Catherine?

Emily: It was a good one.

P: What was so good about it?

Emily: She had a good heart.

P: What do you think you learned most?

Emily: Service, selfless. I did adequately.

I move her over to the state just after death.

P: Where are you now in relation to the body you left behind?

Emily: Above it. The daughters are there.

P: What are you aware of, how are you feeling?

Emily: A big bright light. Anticipating to go home.

P: How do you feel about your death?

Emily: Nothing.

P: Do you wish to remain a while longer to say goodbye to someone or complete some unfinished business on earth?

Emily: I'm ready to go.

Already aware of a light that is guiding her home, I quickly and easily help her cross over to a life-between-life state. She describes how a bright blue light nearby takes the shape of a human form, in a robe, familiar, with a distinctly male and intense energy. She describes him as somebody she has known for a very long time and who has a particular sense of humor. As the guide welcomes her home, she feels a strong sense of relief and safety. She follows the guide into a bright cathedral-like room with a large curved table at the end, with several large white forms sitting behind it.

P: Is this what we regard as the Council?

Emily: Yes.

P: Where is your guide?

Emily: He's behind me.

P: What happens next?

Emily: I move to the front. In the middle in front of the table.

P: How many shapes are here?

Emily: There are twelve. There's no faces, just white columns.

P: Is there anyone that is stepping forward as the leader of this group?

Emily: One does. He takes on more of a yellow color as he steps forward. Like my guide, he has a kind of halo around him.

P: What is the first impression you receive?

Emily: I feel like I was given a life that wasn't very hard.

P: What do they say in terms of evaluation of the life you just lived as Catherine?

Emily: They are pleased. I enjoyed being of service. There is another Council member stepping forward, he is bigger. He seems to take over the conversation.

P: Are they offering anything in terms of positive criticism about your life as Catherine?

Emily: I dealt well with the loss of my husband. I didn't let it slow down my work. They say one must keep living (*emotional now*). It's an analogy to this life (*her current life as Emily*).

P: Tell me more.

Emily: When you lose somebody you have to let go. Because it is not permanent. It's temporary. You have to learn to separate the two lives.

P: Do you mean separating the life on earth and the eternal life as a soul?

Emily: Connect to the Higher Self more. And move forward with the lessons.

P: What kind of lessons?

Emily: To enlighten others. To the true essence of our being.

P: How does the counsel advise she do that?

Emily: So much suffering could be alleviated if others knew what I knew. But so many people are stuck. In a different mindset. They are fear-based. It's a challenge when you live in a fear-based society to get anybody to listen. It is a hard thing to do because people may think you are unstable because you don't think like them.

P: Yet the Council is suggesting it would be a good thing for you to do, correct? If I understand this correctly from what I'm hearing, would the message be centered about your personal story? Could it be used as a tool to connect with others?

Emily: Yes. It's a way to allow people to understand that there is so much more. Religion is a barrier to understanding. It's helpful to a point. But it's about helping people understand our true existence.

P: What else does the Council offer in terms of advice and encouragement?

Emily: Find like minds. Spiritual people who can access.... Higher people. It will open doors.

P: So they suggest to find your tribe?

Emily: Yes. This tribe will show me how. Find a group that will show me how to help the people that need help.

P: How would the Council evaluate your current life as Emily? Who is stepping forward?

Emily: The yellow one. Approval, if that's the right word, that I have recognized the need for hard lessons.

P: Is that in relation to the loss you experienced?

Emily: Different kinds of losses. Not all losses are death. They teach you the most. It's the ability to see a loss for what it is and the ability to let it go.

P: Please explain.

Emily: Like the loss of my husband. If I hadn't lost him,

I wouldn't have looked for a higher purpose. Loss takes you out of your comfort zone. It makes you look if you are willing to look. The purpose is growth and to help others grow at the same time. If we don't grow, we don't progress. It's about moving into another level.

P: Growing into what or where?

Emily: It's in our nature to keep wanting to grow. To experience and move higher. Beyond this earth.

P: What is Emily's purpose?

Emily: This one has the ability, if she chooses, to help others become enlightened.

P: How is she doing in this regard?

Emily: It's easy to walk away. Choose the hard way instead. It's not what it appears to be. It's not just hard for the sake of hardship. It has a purpose. Because stepping out of that comfort zone is what allows you to connect to a higher reality. The ego tries to be in control because it likes the comfort of a life that doesn't change. She needs to learn to put the ego aside.

P: Where is that ego coming from?

Emily: Society. To be different you stand out. The ego doesn't want to stand out. It's easier to remain anonymous. The ego wants to maintain the status quo, whereas the Higher Self wants to break free.

P: In relation to living several lifetimes around the topic of loss, what can the Council offer in terms of insight?

Emily: We live many lifetimes. Each one is an opportunity to look at things differently, to react to it differently. I'm learning to understand why different things happen. The choice is mine to accept the challenge or not. No judgment.

P: How do you feel about this?

Emily: A little bit of sadness. That it takes a loss to wake up.

P: Now that you experienced these losses, and it has helped you wake up, do we have to perpetuate these losses to continue to learn or are there now other ways to keep growing?

Emily: I can achieve great joy in helping others. I need to leave it behind. It fulfilled its purpose. Holding on to grief can become a habit too. Like a best friend. But that friend at some point can become a real burden.

P: Is there anything we may have missed that the Council may want to add.

Emily: They say that you can let somebody go without ceasing to love them. Letting go is in and by itself a lesson. It's not a betrayal. Others have their own lessons and their own journeys. It's not a bad thing to leave them. Because you're not really leaving them. Don't feel any guilt when you let somebody go. You're not leaving them behind. You're just moving on.

P: Yes, that idea is really based on the notion we only live once.

Emily: Yes, it's a learning experience. Guilt serves no purpose. You can acknowledge your past together and then move on.

What is exceptional about this case are the different ways Emily looks at the meaning of suffering; the alternative ways of looking at loss as well as how to break free from the pain and suffering that comes with it. She shares how a limited belief system based on established religious ideas can become a prison that we hesitate to break free from. In other words, a society or a certain group of people can hold onto limiting or narrow religious and societal dogmas about loss and suffering. By refusing to separate themselves from this collective mindset, because it is seemingly hard or unpopular to do so, people unwittingly remain shackled by them. Some of these limited viewpoints arise from the discomfort with the idea that we have lived many lives before. They are also created due to the incapacity to consider that we are not sinners but are a divine soul made in the image of God reincarnating to eventually become free and divine ourselves.

She instead suggests that we learn to regard our true nature as essentially divine. And that our life on earth is a mere exercise program to break free. To one day, either here on earth itself or in the afterlife, express the true freedom and bliss of spiritual enlightenment.

Her explanation of how the ego is really the minds' way of remaining attached to what is familiar, even when this familiarity causes us so much suffering, is beautiful. In this case, familiarity means limited belief systems. She also refers to fear. What she means here is the fear of change. Fear to make an inner change because it is uncomfortable, but also a fear to disagree with or stand out from the collective mindset of people around us.

This case brings up an important insight into how loss can be a catalyst for growth and change. In order to fully understand this, we have to delve into the mechanics of the subconscious mind. In the world of subconscious science, the subconscious is regarded as a 5-year old child. It is also a habit machine that does not like change. Its function is to protect us and it will stubbornly, like a child, hang on to what it knows and likes until it likes something better. For instance, when you want to take a child's favorite doll away, you may have to offer a large lollypop first, otherwise, the child won't give it to you. In fact, once the child feels threatened by the idea that you want to take the doll away, it will hold on to it even more. So, we need to offer an attractive substitute.

In this example, the substitution of something more alluring, like the lollypop, helps the subconscious child go beyond the need for self-preservation, as it generally only accepts a new solution if it perceives a gain. The subconscious also likes increments and numbers. Just like a child knows that two is more than one, so the subconscious understands what is more and better preferring more over less. The subconscious mind also responds well to metaphors and understands its deeper meaning. It avoids pain at all cost. The subconscious avoids change because change can be painful. Instead, it will keep repeating what it already does endlessly, unless there is an incentive to act otherwise, even if from a conscious standpoint, it may be considered a detrimental behavior. The subconscious doesn't consider behaviors detrimental per se because it perpetuates behaviors until a better incentive or alternative whose benefits are yet to be known are offered to change them.

The above example of a lollypop is a positive incentive. Loss can be another kind of incentive; however strange this may sound. When faced with loss, the incentive to change will only take place if less pain can be experienced by changing, rather than continuing to suffer in its current situation.

Let me give you an example. Imagine a young lady lives with a terrible alcoholic who regularly beats and scolds her. Anybody who knows about her and her situation would advise her to leave this man. But what they don't know is that her father was also an alcoholic who beat her mother and that she was raised in an abusive household. However terrible this situation may seem, her mind was 'conditioned' by abuse. Her subconscious mind, in her early childhood, 'learned' that relationships mean abuse. It is known to her.

Unconsciously she attracted what she already knew, abuse. Since the subconscious mind doesn't like change, it will attract and maintain that what it already knows, in this case, abuse. It feels 'comfortable' this way.

In order for her to leave this abusive relationship, her subconscious mind will need to make a change. So what does it take to change a subconscious mind that doesn't like change? In this case, the pain to change has to be less than the pain to further endure the abuse. So the 'gain' is less pain. Thus, loss can help us change. When the pain of loss is so terrible that even adhering and adapting to established religious and social culture won't provide adequate relief, the mind will start to look for a better belief system. It has to if it wants to avoid this pain.

It is at this point that we become open to a new way of thinking. We start to look for answers that are beyond common opinions and customs. We discover that popular culture doesn't provide us with the depth of understanding that is required to deal with our pain.

People not willing to look deeper, while their suffering is real, actually subconsciously perceive a secondary gain which is the satisfaction their mind perceives from obeying the established order. This secondary gain makes them hold onto their current belief system.

The satisfaction comes from the desire to fit in, be proper, or to be a good member of society or a church group. So the suffering in a way becomes a friend. A familiar voice. None of this happens consciously. You can't blame anybody for this nor force anybody to change. Subconsciously, there is still sufficient perceived support remaining for not making the change. This becomes the double-edged sword of their suffering. Subconsciously they can't make the change to lift themselves out of the suffering completely.

Emily made the change. Loss has awakened her to the

awareness that she is indeed more than a woman who works as a nurse and is now widowed. She has come to understand that she is an eternal soul, traveling from life to life, till one day she may attain enlightenment and freedom. She has come to understand that the losses she faced have helped her realize that nothing is permanent and that the only permanent reality is the divinity of her soul. And that to help awaken others to this incredible message is her path forward to living a life inspired by love and light.

She redefined what love means to her. She now has an unshakable love pillar. Love that is attached to a higher meaning.

Chapter 9

You Are Not Crazy

Anthony came to see me after a life long struggle with excessive marijuana and alcohol use. At twenty-eight years old, he was doing much better, but in his intake questionnaire, he described his struggle to find his true purpose in life. His comments hinted that he had a deep and philosophical mind but was struggling to cope. He mentioned his difficulty dealing with the many external impulses, incessant data processing and expectations society thrust upon him.

When the session induction started he displayed all the characteristics of a somnambulist. A somnambulist is a hyper-sensitive and extra suggestible personality. These types of people are what we call sleepwalkers. They are always in a light hypnotic trance and therefore hyper-suggestible to impulses from the outside world. Their minds are wide open, without the normal filters and safeguards most people have to ward off external impressions.

It is understandable that such a soul will feel overwhelmed by life, as everything that happens is directly absorbed and needs to be internally processed.

A more typical mind develops a 'filter' that is formed around the age of eight to nine years' old which prevents us from remaining completely open and suggestible to outside influences. As young children we don't have this filter, which is a good thing (providing our caregivers are positive influences), so we can learn from our caregivers and quickly absorb everything they have to offer. Before we develop this filter there is no real distinction between a conscious and subconscious mind, and we have one open mind. This filter forms after we have received some teachings from parents, the environment, coaches, and perhaps some spiritual do-s and don't-s. This filter splits the mind into two parts, leaving a subconscious mind of about ninety percent and a relatively small conscious mind of about ten percent.

The subconscious mind maintains the same uncritical childlike nature as before the filter developed, only now it is protected by this filter. The logical and thinking mind is the conscious mind. This mind thinks and rationalizes. As information passes from the conscious mind to the subconscious mind it passes through the filter, which distorts or alters it.

In fact, all the information that comes through our sensory channels (what we see, hear, smell, taste, and touch) is not only distorted but deleted and generalized. As we stated earlier, according to Neuro-Linguistic Programming (NLP), we don't see the reality at all (the 'territory'), only a mere map of it. When information passes via our senses to the mind we delete some of that information. We overlook things or omit them, otherwise, we would be completely overloaded by information. When you look at a painting you mainly register the image and emotions it evokes, but you wouldn't notice the thousands of brush strokes.

We tend to delete things that are not corresponding to what is already known by our subconscious mind. When for example we watch a TV debate between two opposing parties, we automatically dismiss all the arguments of the opponent, however logical and accurate, because his kind of logic is unknown and therefore uncomfortable to us. Our mind won't accept the new information and likes to stick with what it knows, in this case, the opinions of the presenter that corresponds with our own preconceived notions.

We also distort sensory data when we make a misrepresentation of reality. In the case of the TV debate, we rationalize the arguments that are closest to our own ideas and twist these in our favor.

And we generalize, drawing global conclusions based on just a few experiences. Certain media outlets are experts at exploiting this phenomenon to create a bias against particular racial groups by repeatedly highlighting isolated incidents. The mind is easily influenced by such generalizations. This tendency to generalize is not only bad but can also be positive when we take whatever little information we have and draw general conclusions. Think of a scenario where we have to make quick decisions based on just a bit of data.

Anthony's somnambulistic tendencies, therefore, explained some of his issues, especially his incapacity to cope with the noise of the world, and his struggle to adapt. He couldn't easily delete excessive incoming data like most of us can. It is not uncommon for such a sensitive soul to want to drown this noise out by intoxicants.

But the session ended up highlighting something much more important. Namely, that in his search for purpose and in trying to deal with the overwhelming impulses from the world around him, he was reminded of his journey in the past and how his deepest aspirations are actually much more elevated than he was previously aware of. The session re-directed his attention to these highest aspirations and presented him with newfound confidence as well as a new way forward. This case highlights the importance of the pillar of spirituality, and that the absence of it, till now, caused Anthony a lot of pain and grief. During the session, he reconnected with it once again.

P: Tell me what is happening now.

Anthony: I'm behind a desk, I'm writing.

P: Can you describe the room?

Anthony: It's an old building, with stone walls. It's a big desk. There is a small window and it's dark in here. Cold.

P: Tell me more.

Anthony: There is a candle on my desk. I'm wearing a rough cloak, almost like a bag. I'm a friar. A Franciscan. With the rope around my waist.

P: Can you tell me what you are writing?

Anthony: Something spiritual, religious. I'm contemplating and writing. My mind is high.

P: How do you feel?

Anthony: At peace, I like this life.

P: What do you like about it?

Anthony: I have purpose.

P: How would you define this purpose?

Anthony: A life that is aligned with God's purpose for me.

P: Can you help me understand?

Anthony: What can be nobler than living a life that is in alignment with the laws of God.

P: Can you tell me about these laws?

Anthony: The teachings of the sacred scriptures.

P: I see. And you are living accordingly?

Anthony: I'm trying to the best of my ability. Even trying to live this way brings peace and satisfaction.

P: Can you tell me where you are and what date it is?

Anthony: I'm in France, 1630.

P: Can you describe the area for me?

Anthony: It's pretty undeveloped here. My room is part of a large building. It's a wide-open area. We live here together. It's a brotherhood.

After some more descriptions, I end up progressing him to the last day of his life.

P: Can you tell me what is happening, on this last day of your life?

Anthony: I'm tired.

P: How do you feel about the life you just lived?

Anthony: It was a good life.

P: What did you learn?

Anthony: That there is peace when you dedicate your life to a higher purpose. I did well in that regard.

P: If you could change something what would you have done differently?

Anthony: I would have liked a woman. Started a family. But this kind of life won't allow for that.

P: So you regret it then?

Anthony: No, it was unavoidable. It's the choice I made.

P: What is your state of mind?

Anthony: Peaceful, satisfied, a life well-lived.

I now guide him to the life-between-life state. He describes entering a peaceful heaven-like garden where he lays down on a rock. It's a place of healing and restoration. Starting to get disconnected from his life as a friar he starts to reflect on his life as Anthony, speaking about him in the third person.

Anthony: Anthony is unsure.

P: Unsure about what?

Anthony: His purpose.

P: What would you advise him to do?

Anthony: He's allowed the ways of the world to intimidate him.

P: What do you mean?

Anthony: He needs to remember who he is and what his real aspirations are.

P: Can you share with me what these are?

Anthony: It's the realization of his true Self.

P: Ok, that's quite a high calling. Are you saying he is not aware of this?

Anthony: Yes and no. Yes in the sense that he knows deep inside that is what he should really strive for, and no in the sense that this aspiration is buried beneath layers of worldly indoctrination.

P: Hence the confusion?

Anthony: This is what he has worked on in previous lives. His conflict in this life arises out of his forgetfulness of this mission.

P: How did he forget?

Anthony: The intoxicants don't help. It creates a cloud of forgetfulness.

P: But why did he get into that to begin with?

Anthony: Over-sensitivity. Sensitivity is good when it brings you closer to the divine. But if you are out of tune it brings you down.

P: So what do you suggest he do?

Anthony: The first step is to stop using any form of intoxicant. To clear the mind. Then he will remember.

P: Can you be more specific?

Anthony: He will remember his life as a friar and he will remember why he is here on earth. What he should do and strive for.

P: And then what?

Anthony: He will stop thinking he is crazy. He is not crazy.

P: Is that what he thinks now?

Anthony: When the ways of the world drown out the light of the Self that is what happens. Particularly when he has known the path towards the light before.

P: It's like a voice within crying for help?

Anthony: He won't be satisfied with what the world has to offer him.

P: Can you help me understand?

Anthony: He feels purposeless because he is seeking for purpose in a world that doesn't resonate with his internal aspirations.

P: Are you saying he is looking in the wrong place?

Anthony: Yes. He gets disheartened and frustrated with the current of the world. He has always found his aspiration and purpose in striving for things that were beyond this world.

P: Hence the intoxicants.

Anthony: It has been an attempt, though unsuccessful, to avoid the world and what he thinks it demands of him. He didn't want to comply.

P: So what is the way forward?

Anthony: Start thinking clearly. The ways of the world and aspiration for transcendental awareness can co-exist.

P: Can you give an example?

Anthony: He doesn't have to give his heart and soul to a career, to make a success of himself in the world. Just work to eat and have a roof over your head. Place the emphasis on realizing this highest Self instead.

P: That sounds like good advice.

Anthony: Nobody forces you to be worldly-minded. That is his fundamental mistake.

P: To not be more strong in his own aspirations?

Anthony: You have to be true to the calling of your own heart. Not let the world around you intimidate you. He must stand up and be stronger.

P: As a summary, what would you advise him specifically?

Anthony: First stop drinking and smoking weed. This will clear up his mind. When the mind is clear he will start to remember his true calling. He can hang on to that. Take confidence in knowing that all along his intentions have been right. That he doesn't have to go the same route everybody else seems to be traveling and that instead, he can create a life for himself that allows him to work toward realizing his truest potential, setting his true Self free.

P: Integrating his highest aspirations with living a smooth life in the world.

Anthony: Yes, he will do this. He is ready.

It is so common that we misunderstand these sensitive souls. It is not that we need to condone intoxicant behavior, but often we misdiagnose or are unaware of the depth of their feelings. Particularly in our modern world, there isn't much in terms of guidance or inspiration that can lead us to live a life in tune with spiritual principles. It's a sad reality that many sensitive people feel tremendously alone and lost amidst a powerful current of worldly ambitions.

It is my hope that we can enlighten our youngsters and

show them that there is no need to hide their intuition and true identity. Instead, we can encourage them to build a life and culture for themselves where these principles are appreciated and lived.

Anthony had to travel a difficult path. Had he been guided and supported when he was young and had there been a culture around him that would have understood his feelings, things could have worked out so much differently. Instead, he had to suffer through intoxication and loneliness. Thankfully, he managed to get his act together before the world swallowed him up completely.

I have witnessed a similar phenomenon in many clients of incompatibility with or deep struggle of the soul to adapt to our modern world. Much like in Anthony's case, the way and culture in which they lived in past lives, is almost opposite to the environment to which they have to adapt to in this life.

Interestingly, when reconnected to higher consciousness, they are advised to become aware of their previous attainments in earlier lives and to learn to adapt to this life. Not to become conditioned and indoctrinated by it, but to create an awareness of their true Self, their true journey, in spite of living in this world.

The world around us cannot be an excuse for failing to manifest our highest spiritual aspirations. Instead, we have to live in such a way that we cultivate sufficient strength and awareness to elevate our consciousness above it, while still being able to function in it.

True awakening is when we are awake in this life and beyond this life. It is a misconception that heaven or liberation is a place beyond this one.

If you're not awakened here, you won't be awakened there either. You can't run away. Awakening, awareness, needs to be attained in the here and now. True, the life-between-life state is a much freer and more elevated state than our life on earth, but it is still subject to conditioning. We still project it into existence. Without being completely awakened we will need to come back and keep on living till the day comes where we won't make any more distinction between living a life here on earth or in the afterlife. Our consciousness will be liberated regardless of what plane of existence we dwell.

This is an important lesson because it is a human tendency to defer our efforts to become awakened to the future. We think it is sufficient to just believe or to just belong to the right church or tradition. Or we hope that when we die and enter the afterlife things will get better. In other words, there is nothing we need or can do right now. We sort of give up.

Instead, as the guides from the life-between-life state keep telling us if we would learn to live free now and bring the enlightened consciousness down to earth, we could enjoy ourselves so much more. Imagine a group of people or a community where souls are awake to the true nature of their higher Self. They would create a world where children are encouraged to develop their higher faculties. They would create a world with a proper balance between love, safety, and spirituality.

Even if we fail to build such a society collectively, nothing stands in our way to create our own household this way and teach our children accordingly. An important lesson from Anthony's case is that, first and foremost, we need to cultivate the strength to do so. With that strength and confidence, we build our vision and reach for the stars. This life is just a passing phenomenon. Why allow it to overwhelm us so much that we forget who we truly are and what we came here to do. If there is anything to be learned from all of this, it is the fact that our true essence is divine, and that our life in this world is a mere training program to set us free. This realization, if truly lived, will provide us the required strength and courage to stand up and build a beautiful life here on earth, fully awake, yet completely integrated. A strong spiritual pillar.

Anthony learned that success is not measured in terms of having a great career and that there is no need to have one. He realized he isn't crazy for not wanting to pursue what most people are pursuing. That instead he wants and needs to live a spiritual life, and that the forgetfulness of his divine mission is what caused him all this pain.

Each of these three pillars is a purpose in and by itself. Striving to attain a perfect balance between them is an even higher purpose. The highest purpose, when all three are in balance, is to come to a state of spiritual awakening.

Chapter 10
Shifting The Paradigm

If we have to choose one of the most important recurring themes in the past-life and life-between-lives regressions it must be the idea of growth. The very purpose of past life regression is to determine the events and patterns out of our past that have contributed to our growth. The karmic lessons we learn through repeated rebirths are there to help us develop and manifest our higher faculties, so that one day we may start to express true divine qualities.

Though the main purpose behind reincarnation seems

to be a singular idea, namely the the awakening of our true Self, the lessons are very individual in nature. We're each on a different level requiring unique lessons that are specifically designed for our individual growth. Some of us need to first strengthen, one, two or perhaps even all three pillars first. We may have to dedicate one or multiple lives to strengthening just one of these pillars. This then becomes a sub-purpose in the grand scheme of our soul's overall purpose, our journey towards awakening.

During a life-between-life regression, we repeatedly witness the soul being instructed on how to further its development. The past life regression highlights the patterns and lessons learned so far, and the life-between-life regression instructs us how to move forward from here. It is important therefore to become aware of both of these lessons; to understand the patterns of the past and to move forward into the future.

Though each lesson is specifically catered to each individual soul, there seem to be certain principles that apply to all. In the same way that gravity applies to all of us, principles and laws of the universe equally apply to us all, even in the afterlife. Think of the law of karma, for example. You can't disconnect reincarnation from the law of karma. This law governs the results of our actions. We reincarnate as a result of our actions and to work out these karmas.

If we consider it acceptable that parental influence, environmental condition, and hereditary transmission is what makes us who we are today, it is just as logical that the law of karma determines why we are born with these parents, in this environment, and with this body. It seems more logical to accept a cosmic intelligence behind this process than to merely leave this to be the results of random luck. Because if it is random, some people have been dealt a great deck of cards, whereas others never had a chance to begin with. It seems fairer to attribute it to the workings of the law of karma and to have a sense of responsibility. Unless we are part of the problem, we can never be empowered to be part of the solution. When you look at life through the lens of karma, what initially may seem like a raw deal, may in the grand scheme of things, be something that we ourselves chose to help us grow.

For example, we may have chosen a difficult family dynamic because it challenges us to become more independent, or we may choose to live in a body with certain challenges to quickly pay off large chunks of karma. What at first glance may look like an unfair situation may, from a higher perspective, be a deliberate and intelligent step taken by the soul to accelerate its growth.

It may require a paradigm shift to accept this kind of thinking. We instinctually believe that we are here on earth to enjoy ourselves. We go to school, get a job, get married because we believe this is what is going to make us happy. It is uncommon for anybody to sit down at an early age and thoroughly investigate this state of affairs. It's something that we collectively have accepted life to be and it's like a strong and powerful current we get swept away with from the day we are born. Anybody refusing to comply with this state of affairs is considered an antagonist, an abnormal person or antisocial.

If you look at this world and the way we live from the perspective of the life-between-lives world, and if the main theme seems to be that we are here to grow, then maybe those that question the way we live are not that abnormal after all.

I remember as a kid asking these questions. I also had an unusually strong unwillingness to comply with the ways of the world. I didn't particularly express this in an aggressive or antisocial way. It was more of an internal struggle. I attempted to make sense of things philosophically, trying to find answers that made sense to me and that would help me chart a course in life I would be able to navigate willingly.

Remembering some of my past lives helped me do this. My acceptance of the idea of karma came to me as a result of this remembrance, as it was the only idea that made sense to me that explained why I was here today and why I was who I was at this point in time. It also made me aware that I had a choice. A choice to craft my life in such a way to help me manifest greater levels of inner freedom.

Consequently, I felt I had to make certain decisions that were not in line with the collective mindset of the society. It so happened that at a young age I came in contact with certain Indian holy men who helped me shape my mind and influenced me to become a monk. And so after college, I spent the next 21 years as a Vedic monk, living all over the world, meditating and giving lectures on Eastern philosophy. It was a wild ride. I'm glad I had the opportunity to live with such great souls, and when most of them passed away I decided to leave the monastic life and explore different aspects of life.

I have no regret living the monk's life, yet I'm happy to have moved on from that as well. It helped me look at life from a more transcendental and detached vantage point. It helped me stop, sit down and reflect before I entered life in the world blindfolded. The monk's life was a great way to internalize my unwillingness to comply with the ways of the world and gave me time to be away from the world and make sense of it.

The incredible brotherhood was also something unforgettable. I will especially never forget the two years I spent in seminary in Kolkata. The spiritual bond that formed between us can never be erased, even though I've chosen to live a spiritual life on my own, away from organized religion. Some of these brothers still visit me in dreams. They are really beautiful divine souls and I will always be grateful to have spent these unforgeable years in their holy company. I resonate with the native woman in the case described below, where she highlights the beauty of sharing spiritual ideas with a group of like-minded souls. For me though, the monk's life, however much I enjoyed it for as long as it lasted, was just a phase. I eventually ended up choosing a lifestyle that allowed me more freedom. It greatly helped me at the beginning of my spiritual life but became increasingly restrictive as

I grew. When a young sapling is planted you may want to put a fence around it so the sheep won't eat the leaves. But once the tree has grown you can tie ten sheep to it and it can even provide shelter against the hot sun. It all depends where you are on the spiritual path. Nothing is good or bad in and by itself. It's an art to learn to be authentic to the needs of your heart and make the required adjustments.

We don't want to get lost in the world. Ideally, we learn to live a life where early on, when we are still young, we are awakened to the higher purpose of life, namely the awakening of our true divine potential and the manifestation of higher consciousness. The art is not to get caught by getting so preoccupied with the things of the world that we completely forget our divine purpose and divine nature.

That is living the enlightened life. The paradigm shift is to learn to enjoy life in a different way. The pursuit of enjoyments we normally regard as the goal of life is to be subordinated to the pursuit of the divine inner bliss of our higher consciousness.

The pursuit of the things of the world may keep us stuck to lower consciousness and eat up all our resources, both internally and externally. Remember the diagram on happiness. All we do is eat the same piece of chocolate over and over again, repeating the same mind wave, without lifting the quality of happiness, and spending a lot of time and energy doing it.

If instead, we learn to understand that we are here to do greater things, manifest greater levels of happiness while lifting our minds into higher levels of consciousness, we can create a better society and a happier life.

We can learn to re-evaluate the things we do and live life differently. The goal is still to experience happiness here on earth but of a different and higher kind. Rather than seeking happiness in an accumulation of ever-increasing material affluence, which is not sustainable, we can seek happiness within our minds and hearts instead. That's the essence of the paradigm shift. Spend less time and energy building extravagant material wealth and spend more time building a brilliant and enlightened mind. Joy originates in the mind.

It is not that our internal push for enjoyment is wrong, but that we place the emphasis on something that cannot deliver that kind of happiness. We need to shift the emphasis from increasing the quantity of happiness to the quality of happiness.

It is true that this isn't easy. We have been so tremendously conditioned. Everybody around us is running after more material wealth, thinking that the more money we have the happier we will be. I'm not advocating that poverty is a virtue. Far from it. In our triangle of a balanced life, i.e. safety, spirituality and love, money is a critical element. It is an aspect of the pillar of safety required to create a life of freedom. However, we need to shift from money-minded consciousness to awakened consciousness. Money and comfort is just a part of it, not all of it. Accordingly, we need to spend only the required time and energy on it and dedicate the rest of our time and energy pursuing other aspects required for living a balanced life.

This brings me to the next case. It illustrates how a life of affluence has disconnected this lady from her larger spiritual purpose. She had overemphasized the pillar of safety, at the expense of love and spirituality. Sharon was a 45-year-old lady from Virginia that came to see me in my office. Having an intelligent and outgoing personality, it was easy to connect with her. She had written to me earlier that she was looking to connect to a higher consciousness but that she had a hard time doing so. Dissatisfied with the goings-on in her life, she was looking for a divine connection. I effortlessly regressed her to one of her past lives:

P: Are you a man or a woman?

Sharon: A woman.

P: What's your age?

Sharon: 18.

P: What are you wearing?

Sharon: I'm barefooted. I wear a beautiful tan buckskin dress.

P: Anything else?

Sharon: I'm also wearing hand beaded colorful jewelry.

P: Where are you now?

Sharon: In the forest.

P: What are you doing?

Sharon: I'm looking out over my tribe.

P: What are you looking at?

Sharon: I'm looking at the smoke rising up from the fire. It's evening. The sky is full of color. Reds and orange.

P: How are you feeling?

Sharon: So at peace.

P: How come?

Sharon: It's the forest, the way we live.

P: Ok, can you elaborate?

Sharon: We're connected. With nature and with each other.

P: Who are we?

Sharon: My people, my tribe

P: How many are you?

Sharon: 25. We live here together.

Can you describe how you live?

Sharon: We live in woven huts, with thick heavy grass roofs. We're in a clearing in the forest. There is a river nearby. We're surrounded by mountains.

P: How would you describe your people?

Sharon: We're natives. We've lived in these areas for a very long time.

P: Have you always lived here?

Sharon: We do move sometimes, following the buffaloes.

P: What is the main source of sustenance?

Sharon: The men hunt buffalo, deer, and fish. The women gather berries, roots, and herbs for medicine.

P: Can you describe the area?

Sharon: It's beautiful. Large trees. Our huts are under the trees, in a circle. We have a fire in the middle. The women are working, preparing baskets and making food. The men are away, hunting. Some elders remain.

P: How is the climate?

Sharon: It's warm now. But it's a mild climate.

P: You said you are at peace?

Sharon: There is harmony. I feel so happy.

P: What do you mean by harmony?

Sharon: The forest is alive. I can feel it. We listen to it and breath with it. We adapt to it and live with it. We do this as a group.

P: So you're sharing this awareness?

Sharon: Yes, that's what makes our lives so peaceful. We breathe, dance and live as one.

P: What makes you so united?

Sharon: As I said, we breathe as one and the elders guide us.

P: What can you tell me about the elders?

Sharon: They have experience. They have wisdom.

We listen to them.

P: How do they guide you?

Sharon: We sit together at night, around the fire. They tell stories, through song and dance.

After some more descriptions about her life in the tribe, I progress her forward in time a few times. She describes getting older and slowly becoming one of the elders who helps the younger girls. I then guide her through her last day on earth and help her cross over. Here she becomes very chatty and observant, unconditioned from any life.

P: What do you think about the life you just lived?

Sharon: It was a beautiful life.

P: What did you like best?

Sharon: I was in tune.

P: Can you elaborate?

Sharon: The sense of connection was very powerful. Connected with each other and with nature. It was a flow.

P: How is that different in Sharon's life?

Sharon: She's missing that.

P: Why do you think that is?

Sharon: She's neither connected with people or nature.

P: Do you know why?

Sharon: Her affluence has created barriers.

P: What kind of barriers?

Sharon: It's like living in a walled castle. There is an alienation from people and nature. It's unnatural.

P: What do you suggest she do?

Sharon: She needs to simplify her life.

P: How do you suggest she does that?

Sharon: She doesn't need all this stuff, this large house, this gated community. She needs to make a change, live connected.

P: Live connected?

Sharon: Yes, that's why she went back today to visit her past life as a native American. She needed to feel this again. You may think it was a primitive life. But it wasn't.

P: You mean that she needs to rekindle that kind of connectivity with nature and people?

Sharon: Yes, find her tribe, so to speak. Like-minded people who look for things other than material comfort. She's so tired of this.

P: I understand. Why now?

Sharon: Why not now. It is time. She's wasted enough time. She's allowed herself to be engulfed by societies demands. It's stupid.

P: So she's ready to make a change then?

Sharon: She has to. Otherwise, she lives in vain. She's just existing. Having money doesn't change that. It doesn't add anything to how she's been feeling.

P: An interesting observation.

Sharon: What made me happy as a native woman wasn't

material. As a matter of fact, it was just the opposite. It was living with a group of people who understood what makes life meaningful. Being together, sharing an understanding of spiritual principles, having few needs and demands. It's such freedom.

P: Can Sharon recreate such a life?

Sharon: It's not about recreating the past. It's about integrating these principles in today's world.

P: What does that mean in practical terms?

Sharon: Sharon can live in a simple house, close to people or a community that values her ideas. By living simply, she doesn't need to dedicate a huge amount of time and money to uphold her lifestyle.

P: Yes, that makes sense.

Sharon: She will have time to reach out, connect, pursue things that elevate her mind. That's what's important.

P: What does she hope to achieve with this?

Sharon: Happiness. It's a state of mind. You need to create a set of circumstances that allow for this.

P: So you're saying that by simplifying her life, spending less energy on material things, and spending more time with like-minded people she can elevate her mind?

Sharon: Yes. In order for consciousness to unfold the other aspects of one's life need to be properly organized. Otherwise, it's like walking in two different directions at once.

P: Are you suggesting that you can't achieve happiness if the pillars of your life are not set up right?

Sharon: Sharon spends too much time in material comfort and too little time making meaningful connections. By making some fundamental changes in her life she can liberate her mind. Only then can she become happy. Happiness, consciousness, emerges from living the right way. You can't disconnect one from the other. It's a lifestyle. You have to be aware of all these things.

P: Is that what you mean by walking in two different directions at once?

Sharon: Dedicating a disproportionate amount of time and energy to the things of the world is detrimental to achieving a liberated state of mind. You can't expect to have enough energy to achieve both. There needs to be a balance.

P: So you have to make a choice?

Sharon: It's choosing between different kinds of happiness. If you want the things of the world it can bring you a certain kind of comfort, but the price is high. It goes at the expense of peace of mind and meaningful connections. Choosing to live a life in harmony with nature, with like-minded people means giving up a certain amount of material comfort, but you get peace of mind in return.

P: I fear people may misunderstand this, they feel they have to go and live in the forest.

Sharon: That's taking it to another extreme. It's

about balance. We don't need to deprive ourselves of anything. But we need to understand the principles.

P: How would you define these principles?

Sharon: You only have a certain amount of energy. You spend it in pursuit of wealth you will get wealth. If you release some of that energy and dedicate it to connecting to nature and other people that's what you get. If you preserve energy and direct it to meditation and prayer you will get inner peace. It's a simple concept.

P: Yet one that Sharon has been struggling to implement so far.

Sharon: She knows. She just needs a push in the right direction.

In this insightful session, Sharon's higher Self redirected Sharon to live a more enlightened life. Sharon had become stuck in her ways, and her affluence had become a prison for her mind.

Whether you already have money or not, the lesson in this session remains the same. We have been conditioned to run after the things of the world. Comfort, bigger houses, nicer cars, a bigger bank account. Deep in our subconscious mind, the programs have been written. It pushes us in this direction blindly. We don't even question it anymore. Even though very few people are actually truly happy and at peace, and there is no evidence around us that this program is actually delivering the promised land, we relentlessly push on.

In order to change this script, a fundamental change in our mind is needed. We need to rewrite the programs that govern our subconscious mind to make the subconscious conscious. How can we do this?

The first step is to visualize what we want. Create a clear image of the new and improved life you want to live. Then plant this deep into the subconscious mind. Over and over again imagine and visualize, using all of your senses. Make it come alive. See it, smell it, and feel it as if it already happened. As these ideas and visions become alive, they slowly sink down into the most secret recesses of your subconscious mind. Through continuous repetition, this dream forms a new impression within. Believe it or not, the universe will magically make it happen. The universe supplies what you have deep down into your subconscious. It never fails.

This is a secret I have discovered over the years and that I like to share with you here. Once you understand this principle you have a tool that can change your life. I'll show it to you in the drawing below.

1. The 'here and now', your 'reality' as you know it: This is how you experience your life. It is how you feel, stuff that happens to you, people you meet, opportunities or the lack thereof, etc. It's your conscious reality. By conscious we mean that what YOU are conscious of. This implies that there are forces at work that you are NOT conscious of. It's the amazing characteristic of our conscious mind that it gives us the illusion that what I am conscious of is all there is and the only thing that is true.

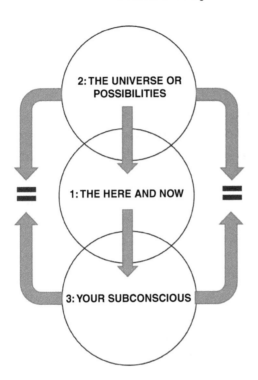

It is that sphere that is characterized by the illusion that as long as I am conscious of it, it must be real and true (or be the only truth). We also dismiss (or as NLP states, delete, generalize or distort) anything that falls outside this realm of what I am conscious of.

2. The Universe, or the unknown: The universe is that mysterious realm that we pray to, expect things from or curse at when we do not get what we want. It is that realm around us with infinite forces of gravity, electromagnetism, strong and weak nuclear forces, light, prana, chi and so forth. It's also the life-between-life consciousness. When we want or desire something it needs to come from somewhere. If we want love, wealth, health, it is reasonable to assume that this abundance is already available in the universe around us even though we are not aware of this. Hence the saying of a great Eastern saint: 'The wind of grace is always blowing; you have to raise your sails.' Though we are part of and live in this universe, its potential lies outside our conscious experience. We are not conscious of these forces surrounding us and it's potential. So rather than calling this circle the universe, we can also call it potential, or possibility.

3.   **The Subconscious Mind:** The vast realm of our mind that we know is there but we can't see. If we want to draw into our conscious reality the things the universe can offer us, then we first need to plant it deep down into the subconscious mind. We can do this through continuous repetition (like the repetition of positive affirmations), meditation, psychotherapy or hypnotherapy. Once an idea becomes a new impression in the subconscious mind, the universe will find a way to make it come to you. The secret is that the supply of the universe is always available but only presents itself into your conscious reality when it first exists in the subconscious mind. *The universe's supply and your subconscious mind are always one and the same.* They need to be attuned. The subconscious frequency needs to be attuned to the frequency of the universal supply. Just like a radio needs to be attuned to the broadcasting tower. If you want life to give you love, then you need to get the love frequency in your subconscious mind first. Do you want affluence? Then you need to get the frequency

of wealth consciousness in your subconscious first. The universe reads these frequencies and tunes into it and returns the favor. Just like the radio.

The same is true with negativity of course. Having depressed and bad thoughts will leave you with a conscious experience of negativity. The universe will return the same frequency to you and bad things start to happen in your life. Understanding this secret allows you to create your own destiny. Suddenly good things start to happen, great opportunities present themselves. It is a coincidence or luck? It is the power of your own subconscious mind.

So change is possible, even if the world around us moves in the opposite direction. All it takes is a conscious intention, then we will find ways to make what you desire happen.

Sharon is ready to make the change. She has now become aware that she over-invested in material comfort (safety pillar) and underinvested in meaningful relations (love pillar) and attaining a higher level of consciousness (spirituality pillar). In order to be happy and at peace now, her immediate purpose is to restore the balance.

Chapter 11
Freedom

One of my fondest memories of living in India was my stay in South India. After more than 7 years in North India, I moved to the southern state of Karnataka. The first time I crossed the border into one of the Southern states an overwhelming sense of joy and recognition came over me. I was taking the Coromandel Express from Kolkata to Chennai and I'll never forget the first stop in what was considered the South, somewhere in Andhra Pradesh. There on the railway platform, I saw the men wearing traditional dhotis (a long cloth that is wrapped around the waist like a skirt) and women with a turmeric concoction smeared on their faces and flowers in their longs braids. Hawkers offered idlis (rice cakes) and doshas (rice flower-lentil pancakes) and I felt at home immediately.

This feeling of familiarity and my appreciation of the Southern Indian culture never left me during my 3 years there. It was clear to me that I lived here before. This feeling became even stronger when for the first time I visited Bangalore, the capital of Karnataka. At the time I was there it was still pretty much the garden city it was traditionally known for, though over the years the IT Industry has overwhelmed the city and it lost some of its charms due to heavy air pollution and overpopulation.

My favorite spot in Bangalore was the Ramakrishna Ashram in the Basavanagudi area. Though I lived most of the time in Mysore, I visited the Bangalore ashram regularly. This sacred spot, a large walled compound amidst trees and well-kept gardens, right in the heart of the city, has a beautiful and intimate temple where devotees can come and attend daily devotions and sacred ceremonies.

It took me by surprise, when I first walked the grounds, how I loved this place and how comfortable I felt here. Nowhere in India did I ever feel such a sense of belonging and ease. The most famous landmark in the ashram is what is called Holy Mother's rock. It is a big granite boulder with a cute little carved mandapa (a pillared cover) and a small shrine dedicated to her visit here some 100 years ago.

I immediately recognized this place. This is where I met

this holy lady during my past life. This moment brought me back to my childhood when I had a vivid dream of this place. I clearly remember walking up the rock, along with other devotees, when one by one we offered some sacred items to her. I remember giving her a beautiful white flower and a saffron robe (traditional monk's robe), which she gave back to me as a blessing. When years later I lived with an Indian saint near Paris I told him about this dream. He got up, pulled a book off the shelf and opened it up showing me the exact description of my dream. 'This is where you were,' he told me. I had up to that point never heard of Bangalore or of this incident.

Now, visiting this rock I realized why I felt so comfortable here. This particular ashram is also the place where my mind was at its best. I would easily and effortlessly enter a high state of consciousness. Though some of the more traditional and conservative Indian ascetics living in this place regarded me as a white and 'unspiritual' foreigner, my mind was flying high here. I remember this one particular day during a busy and large religious festival with sacred ceremonies going on in the temple. I was sitting absorbed in a high state of peace on a wall in the garden just outside the temple, when of these conservative ascetics urged me to come into the temple to attend the ceremony. When I politely declined he walked away irritated at my lack of devotion. I sat there motionless in what seemed to be me staring ahead into a void, completely calm and in internal bliss. I was in a desire-less and wave-less state of consciousness. What could any temple visit contribute to this blissful state of being?

To this day I smile at the miraculous play of destiny. We travel from life to life, from culture to culture and from lifestyle to lifestyle. Each time a different role, a different era. But it is possible to remember some of these travels and when we do, we start to discover a wonderful and mysterious journey unfolding through time and space. What I am learning from this journey is that I am a free spirit. I was this monk, this family man, this blacksmith, this soldier, but these were just roles I played. When consciousness unfolds, we become aware that in and through all these roles we are a divine spirit that is always free, that can always be happy, irrespective of the external circumstances we may find ourselves in this time around.

The external circumstances don't really matter all that much. Our station in life is less relevant when we remember who we really are. It doesn't matter whether you are a man or a woman, a monk or a family man, rich or poor, black or white, gay or straight. You have been all of these before already. What matters is to remember who you really are and that through playing these roles you learn to love, to understand and finally, to transcend.

When I was sitting there on that wall the cultural differences between me and the people around me didn't matter to me. The background in religious affiliation didn't matter. My skin color didn't matter. Being misunderstood didn't matter. These may have been issues in the minds of other people around me but in my elevated state of consciousness these where just clouds passing by. Primarily I felt a sense of light, bliss, and freedom within.

These states come and go and it takes a lot of time and effort to learn to stay continually in this kind of mind space. But even then it showed me the benefit of living a spiritual life. No matter what happens, when your mind is in the right place you can be happy. Our state of consciousness is what matters most.

What is required though, as we discussed in an earlier chapter, is to set up one's life in such a way that it is conducive to maintaining this state. Love, our need for safety, and spirituality need to be balanced. It is the platform upon which higher states of consciousness can be sustained. When we neglect to take care of these things our life becomes unstable and we will be distracted and uneasy. It is impossible to maintain a carefree and high state of mind when this happens. The foundation needs to be rock solid first. As the Bible says, you cannot build a house on sand. Higher consciousness is not just a state of mind; it requires a lifestyle.

I have found that it isn't enough to just have a glimpse of such a state once in a while. What if I could remain in such a state and it became my nature, my default mode? My personal ideal has always been freedom. This is a work in progress, especially since my idea of freedom constantly changes. It is hard to define in certain terms what man's goal is here on earth. It's different for everybody. When we look at how many lives we all live, it is pretty obvious we are at different stages on our journey. One person may have traveled through many more lifetimes than another. Even within this life itself, we go through stages and constantly evolve while our needs at any given moment change. So even if you could define the goal of life as one single thing, we would still be at different stages in relation to that goal.

Let's say for argument's sake that spiritual freedom would be the goal of mankind. Even if this would be the case, not everybody would be immediately aware of this. One's immediate short term goal would be dependent upon where one is in relationship to this goal. When there is a certain desire that needs to be worked out in a particular lifetime, and if this desire stands in the way of attaining true freedom, then it would be of paramount importance to first fulfill this desire; to know and experience what the nature of this desire is; to taste it, live it and accordingly draw our own experiential conclusion about it. Fulfilling this desire would be the foremost thought in your mind. It would consume you and most probably you wouldn't think much past this desire. And, you wouldn't really be able to cross the hurdle of this desire without first thoroughly understanding the nature of it. You can't repress or suppress it away. It will come back later and you'll have to deal with it at another time.

Accordingly, we all have different goals depending on these desires we encounter on the path towards freedom. As and when we fulfill certain desires, and understand the consequences of our actions, we move on to the next stage. With each desire fulfilled the mind learns, changes and matures.

When I was a young teenager, my desire for freedom

expressed itself through being against what everybody else was doing. The idea to get a job, get married, have a mortgage, live in the same town, and have the same job for the rest of my life terrified me. This reluctance to comply had far and deep-reaching consequences. I didn't know it at the time and hadn't thought it through completely and it was still an immature and rebellious expression of what I felt deep inside.

At first, it expressed itself through simple things, like not wanting to use alcohol, even though everybody around me did. Or fighting for what I regarded was the truth, in a very aggressive and self-righteous way. I would engage in lengthy discussions with people whom I thought had done something wrong and would try to either convince them of my truth or try to subjugate them with my intellect. This attitude didn't make me a very popular figure, especially since I was clever with words.

Of course, this ended up causing me more trouble than it was worth and left me without friends for a while. What was good about it was that it made me want to get out of my town as quickly as I could. Had I not been so radical I would most probably still be there today and not have been able to reach out and see the world.

As I matured a bit through college I started to re-direct my non-compliance with the world towards starting to improve myself instead. My earlier attitude had left me unhappy and displeased with myself and I needed help. During these 5 wonderful years at the Design Academy in Eindhoven, Holland, I met wonderful and artistic souls who came from all over the country. Away from my hometown and surrounded by creative and freedom-loving people, I started to blossom slowly. It is during this time that I met the Indian holy men I mentioned earlier in this story.

These beautiful beings helped me change my attitude. They made me aware that fighting the world was not going to do much for my state of happiness. They pointed out it would be far more intelligent to fight the negative thoughts in my mind and turn these towards constructive and positive ones. They taught me early on that to take care of my body, my mind and spirit would help me feel and function better. It was a simple concept, but I understood that with a better-equipped body and mind I would perhaps be able to create a future for myself where I'd be free and live on my own terms.

Rather than fighting an external world that would forever be out of my control, I could create an internal environment where I am in control.

Hanging out with these Indian holy men left me deeply impressed by their love and wisdom. I also noticed an internal happiness in them that I couldn't detect in many others around me. I wanted to emulate that. So after finishing college and getting my degree in Industrial Design I ripped the hard-fought-for document in pieces, dumped all my projects in the garbage, shredded my portfolio and joined an ashram in France. Radical still.

Though my parents supported what I did (they were

radical in their own way and could appreciate me trying to find my own way), nobody else appreciated this move. They couldn't understand how I could throw away such a valuable career and thought I had gone crazy. Funny enough, even today, decades later, people in my hometown still think I joined an oriental cult.

I never really cared about what anybody thought of me. What was important to me was trying to come to a state of mind and developing a way of life where I felt free. Joining an ashram in France was what at the time felt freest to me. Surrounded by sincere and spiritually-minded souls was a great time and living with holy company lifted my mind.

As time went by though things gradually changed. The change was slow and almost imperceptible. Early on living in the ashram I became attracted to the idea of being a monk, a sanyasi, and spent a lot of time and energy preparing for this mission. It is this desire that brought me to India where I could learn at the source. Slowly, being preoccupied with being a monk became more important than living a simple and pure spiritual life. As time went by the duties and responsibilities of organized religion started to dominate my life. I had, unbeknownst to myself, created a whole new set of bondages.

Of course, living as a monk wasn't a waste of time. Instead of being occupied day and night with family affairs and making money, I had the opportunity to study sacred scriptures and meditate on the banks of the Ganges and in remote temples in the Himalayas. Not just for a few weeks but years on end. It does something within. It changes you for the better.

An added advantage of living in a radically different culture like India was that it completely ripped me away from everything I had known so far. In a place like India, everything is different. The food, the climate and, most importantly, the culture. You don't have anything you know and feel comfortable with to rely on. You have to rely on something solid within. However much I loved India and the monks' life, I never wanted to be an Indian and replace my cultural and European identity with another one. I was open to investigate my European conditioning and make changes, but not at the expense of being my authentic self. I was here to learn and expand, not to become an Indian. This stubbornness, again, is what made the people in my predominantly Indian religious tradition uneasy. They wanted me to comply. What they didn't understand was that over the years I had become a master of non-compliance, but now, instead of openly arguing, I had found ways of trying to get what I needed without openly displeasing the people around me. I was here willingly, trying to learn, study, absorb, without getting caught up completely in yet another set of circumstances.

It was still a struggle though. It was only after 10 years in India that I finally came to a place where I was neither a European nor an Indian. I had found something within myself where I could appreciate the best of both cultures without being one-sided and predominantly one or the other. Not that it matters if you are one or the other. But my idea was freedom and that included freedom from cultural indoctrination as well. Not being against anything, but being able to be flexible and appreciative enough to really understand each culture's best features without having to become them. Sipping the honey without getting stuck to the honey pot. And, also important, to shed the negative characteristics of each culture that one unconsciously absorbs. It is only by meeting other cultures head-on that we understand the difference. These differences can make us aware of our own one-sidedness and narrowness. India did a lot for me in that regard. It showed me what it meant to be European. What my strengths and shortcomings were in respect to the Indians. I wanted to continue to learn, develop and be open to the strengths of my own and of the Indian culture, or any culture for that matter.

This freedom-loving attitude is what eventually made me leave the monastic world as well. It had served its' purpose for me. Just like the people in my hometown considered me lost and crazy by leaving, so, unfortunately, my monastic brothers couldn't understand why I would leave. They too considered me lost. Within my heart, I deeply loved them and everything they stand for, but it was necessary for me to move on. I needed to face, what Carl Jung describes, the shadow self.

During the last few years as a monk, I became increasingly aware of deeper aspects within my mind that still needed attention. It was easy to dismiss these aspects of my unconscious personality, because according to the principles of my religious tradition I was already on 'the good and noble path.' Especially after some twenty years in the religious order I was now giving classes and public lectures on philosophy and I had people coming to me for counsel and inspiration. In spite of this, I started to feel increasingly trapped by the very thing that was supposed to make me free. I slowly became a tiger trapped in a cage. My meditation and spiritual practices had made me strong, confident and focused. The narrow boundaries of the religious order and the restrictions imposed upon me became increasingly confining. I deeply loved and believed in the spiritual search and the attainment of higher consciousness, but I increasingly felt that the way I was living was becoming more of a burden than a help.

One day as I was sitting alone somewhere in the monastery, I suddenly felt myself transported to a moment after death. I saw myself sitting there in the future, looking back on my life as a monk. A divine presence sat next to me and started talking to me. Jokingly and half sarcastically he said to me: "So, wonderful, this monastic life, yes? Giving lectures, teaching people. Wearing the noble and beautiful orange robes that the devotees in your little insular world so respect and adore. But it's all vanity don't you see? You've become comfortable. It's all too easy for you. People are now starting to appreciate you. They love your counsel, your talks. But, a chain though made of gold is not less strong to bind. If you stay here any longer you will just be deceiving yourself. You will tell yourself that you are walking the sacred path, but deep inside you are ignoring what really needs to be done to set you free. Don't be afraid my child. Move on. If you don't, you will have a return ticket to earth again. You will have to be born again to finish what you didn't have the courage to finish this time. You need to face reality and work out these last things that stand in your way of complete freedom. People are not going to understand. But you will. You will be walking the path towards true inner freedom."

A week later I left the monastery.

When one door closes another one opens. With almost no money and an outdated education, the only one at my side was Jenna, who later on became my wife. Together we started a little holistic center where we taught yoga and sold spiritual paraphernalia. It is here where I decided to go back to college and become a clinical hypnotherapist after reading Dr. Michael Newton's books: 'Journey of Souls' and 'Destiny of Souls'. Now, years later I have faced the shadow self and have become a better man because of it. I have learned to integrate the need for safety, love, and spirituality. In the same way that I tried to get the best out of my European culture and learn from the Indian culture, I have now tried to extract the best from the monastic culture and integrate it into my new life.

I am trying to preserve and nurture what I learned from and developed in my life as a monk, within a new way of life in the world. I discarded what I found limiting and restricting as a monk, and embraced a new way of life where I can be free. The art is to always be wide awake and alert. The moment we become complacent and attached we get stuck.

My story is but one example of how my search for freedom has kept me moving. For that one has to be courageous and honest with oneself. The source of my courage has always been the knowledge that I have lived many lives before and I have tried to make this philosophical principle a living and breathing reality. This is my truth and living according to this truth has positive implications for me. I don't hesitate to let go of what I feel is a burden and what limits my freedom and to accept new and improved ways when I encounter them.

The terrifying idea that we only live once makes us afraid and attached to the things of this world. But when you know you have lived before and will live again you start to focus more on the things that bring you happiness and peace in the long run. You can also let go of the roles you play more easily.

These roles are the masks we wear. These masks are what in Indian philosophy is called the 'limiting adjuncts.' These are the different layers of the onion wrapped around our core identity, the Soul or Self. Each layer is a mask and limits us, hence the term, limiting adjunct. When I think I am a mere man then I cannot identify with women or gay people. When I think I am a European, I cannot identify with an American. When I think I am a Catholic then I cannot and do not want to relate to a Hindu. Each layer restricts me and limits the range of my soul to connect beyond my limited personality. The thinner the layers the bigger my heart and the more I can reach out and identify with the diversity around me. The thicker the layer the more I am identified with my limited identity and the more afraid I will be to interact and identify with you. The more I am identified with my core reality, my Soul, the more courageous and expansive I will be. So you see, knowing you are an eternal soul that travels from life to life has direct benefits. It makes you more expansive, courageous, and loving. And this translates into a higher level of happiness.

When I went through the ceremony to become a monk, ten years after I joined the monastic Order, I didn't take vows. Instead, I sat around the sacred fire and offered sixty-four of these different limiting adjuncts into the fire. This principle is very dear to me and what I try to live by to this day, and most probably will till the end of my days on this earth. You don't have to be a monk to live by this principle. As a matter of fact, for me being a monk was one of these limiting adjuncts that I eventually needed to let go of. I prefer the term yogi. A yogi is one who strives to be free from these limitations. It doesn't matter what your station in life is. Whether you are married and have kids, whether you are straight, gay or trans, whether you are black, brown, white, from Europe, Asia or America, the principle remains the same. The more masks we lose the bigger a personality we will be. Freedom, I have discovered, is being without masks.

Some people who knew me from my monastic days ask me: how can you maintain a spiritual life after leaving the monastery, now that you have to work and make money like everybody else? To that, I say, who says I have to make money like everybody else? Who says I have to work myself to death every day of the week, year after year, hoping that one day in the future I hope to retire and spend a few years in relaxation and rest? Money is only important as a tool. A tool that has its rightful place on the triangle of a balanced life, along with love and spirituality. You only need to make as much money as you need to survive. Money is only required as a form of security and safety. Not much more. If a strong desire for money and luxury had replaced my monastic life then yes, I would have to work day and night. But I don't have that desire. My desire is to be free. I don't need so much money because I know the disproportionate amount of time and energy required to make that kind of money will bind me instead of making me free. Because I value love and spirituality in my life, money only supports that system and does not dominate it. I just need enough to be safe. I understand now that when safety, love, and spirituality are well balanced in my life, the resulting synergy is freedom.

The other day I had a discussion with a young father about this topic and he told me that my ideas were unrealistic. He said that now that he was a father his family needed stability and that he had to work hard to provide for them. I noticed he wasn't much in a listening mood and I didn't feel like saying something he wasn't willing to hear. But in my mind, I thought that he only believes he needs all of these things. He thinks that stability translates to owning a lot of things. He thinks he needs a half a million-dollar home for his family. He feels he needs two $50.000 SUVs, one for himself and one for his wife because all the other parents have them too. He thinks that he needs a plasma TV in each room because that's how the collective subconscious has been programmed by TV advertisement. Stability isn't a financial concept. As a matter of fact, spending too much time and energy acquiring financial wealth impedes stability. The triangle of a balanced life requires the distribution of time and energy to all three aspects; safety, love, and spirituality. Life will be unstable without this equal distribution of energy and your internal being will suffer accordingly.

We have collectively been brainwashed. We actually don't need all of these things. We would be just as happy in a simple house, with a few things, and spend more energy investing in each other doing fun stuff together, than working a disproportionate amount of time to work for things society tells us we need.

What I learned from being a monk that I was happy without a TV and money and by being alone in a room reading a good book. I'm not proposing that anyone needs to be a monk, but we do need to get back to simplicity. This way we can free up time and energy to do other things. We will have time to spend with our loved ones or time to do yoga, meditate and relax.

This kind of thinking is only possible when we are able to think for ourselves and lift our minds beyond the collective mind. Just think for a moment about all the other lives you have lived. Were any of the things you desire today even available then? Looking back over all these lives, what has always been the most important to you? When you died, over and over again, what were your regrets and what were your greatest accomplishments? What did you value then above all other things? I bet it wasn't an SUV or a flat-screen TV.

I bet that when you sat there after you died looking back over your life, you regretted not spending more time with your loved ones. Or you lamented spending too much time worrying over stuff that wasn't important. That instead you should have spent more time and energy investing in things that helped you evolve as a soul.

To keep consuming more doesn't translate into happiness. Our economic model of a healthy economy as a growing economy is fundamentally flawed. Where are the resources coming from to keep it growing continually? If every person on this earth would reach the level of economic wealth Americans have today, we would need four planets to supply the resources. It will be wiser to rethink our ways. We too are responsible for this folly of blindly consuming and wanting more and better things.

What if we would re-evaluate our lives from the ground up and begin to fundamentally investigate why we do what we do and make changes. Start thinking in terms of soul growth rather than economic growth. When we equally share resources and learn to take care of each other we could eliminate so much fear and insecurity while freeing up our mind's resources for higher things. I'm not proposing communism. I'm proposing a mind shift and an awareness that prioritizes the meaningful things that truly translate to inner peace and happiness. The direction we move in now as a collective society has only made us believe we are moving towards happiness, but instead is robbing us of our resources, both internally and economically. It is not sustainable and won't work. We need to wake up. The journey starts with each one of us individually.

Section 3

Awakening To The Meaning
Of Our Higher Purpose

This third and last section shows us what happens when the three pillars of our lives are in purposeful harmony. The accounts of those in this section demonstrate what happens when our consciousness is liberated from earthly attachments and becomes awakened to the true nature of its' own Self.

We learn what such a state actually looks like, how it is experienced and what it will do for us, here-and-now on earth.

Chapter 12
The Fourth State

Veronica is a 52-year-old entrepreneur from North Carolina, youthful looking, spunky and full of life with her sneakers and cropped hair, reminding me of somebody out of Westside story. Most clients contact me after reading Dr. Michael Newton's books, 'Journey of Souls' and 'Destiny of Souls'. She hadn't read either book but had heard about the process and was very interested. Her intake questionnaire described a 'longing' for something more. Though everything in her life seemed to be in order, she felt a sense of disconnect with the people around her as if she didn't belong. She explained that there wasn't anybody in her world she could really talk to. She even felt, not in a suicidal way but more in an existential way, that she didn't really want to be here anymore. She wanted her incarnations to finally come to an end.

During the induction, I noticed that she entered a deep altered state of consciousness quickly and effortlessly. A normal stage of the regression process is the womb regression, where we take somebody back to the time just before birth when they are still in the mother's womb. This can be a very emotional and therapeutically rich experience. The soul is still partially connected to the life-between-life state and gets acquainted with the new body for the journey ahead.

During regressions, it is not uncommon for the soul to enter the life-between-life sphere straight away from the womb, though the traditional route would be to first enter a past life. Veronica described herself ascending from the womb directly to another dimension. Interestingly, this journey wasn't characterized by a lot of visuals. It is important to note that not everybody is equally visual. Some souls describe elaborately detailed scenes and events, whereas others tend to be much more mental in their experience. Over the years I have learned that the latter isn't any less effective or intense. We all have different ways of seeing and understanding things. Some people are visual, some auditory, some kinesthetic, some mental and so on. We're all unique in the way we process and understand things.

As a therapist it is critically important to understand this and adapt accordingly, allowing the client to experience and express things in the way that works best for them. You can't qualify an experience based on the way it is expressed or experienced.

Accordingly, Veronica's description was to the point and devoid of lengthy descriptions. She just found herself 'there'. There was no Guide, Council, or experience of anything other than drifting in a high state of consciousness. For those who have read Michael Newton's books, this may come as a surprise. Most of the accounts recorded in his work describe elaborate worlds, with different stations where the soul stops and processes experiences. But after having conducted many sessions I have witnessed some souls enter a formless and visionless reality. My own life-between-life experience was very similar, so I understand from personal experience what this state is about. Souls of this temperament experience this reality differently. It may not be a conscious choice, but for them, they experience the life-between-life state as an abstract, blissful, ocean of super-consciousness. It is very similar to the way some Eastern schools of philosophy describe the 'fourth' state. The first three states of mind are waking consciousness, dreaming, and dreamless sleep. The fourth state is called 'turiya'. We're all capable of accessing these four states of consciousness. The first three we access daily; the fourth state is more difficult to attain.

Turiya is described as pure consciousness, the background that sustains and transcends these three common states of consciousness. It is a high state of consciousness where one experiences a sense of infinity and formlessness that is free from the dualistic experience as we know it here on earth. It is a state in which we witness our own true Self as beyond limitations, beyond cause and effect, beyond change, blissful, changeless, luminous, immanent in all things and transcendent above all things.

This state of consciousness is what many yogis strive to experience. As I described in a previous chapter, that state is familiar because I have experienced it during meditation. When you enter this state you know it to be truer than the reality we experience here on earth. It is hard to explain and needs to be experienced. It is like describing or analyzing a glass of milk and all its properties. No matter how qualified scientifically you may be, no matter how well you can describe the milk unless you drink the milk you can't taste it or be nourished by it.

It is important to understand that we are capable of accessing this state of consciousness. It is both a 'place' as well as a 'state'. A place in the sense that it takes us away from our day-to-day world as we know it. A state in the sense that it transcends this world and connects us to this infinity beyond name and form, beyond the duality of our world.

Thus when Veronica entered this frequency I immediately knew this is where she was. She had entered the turiya state.

P: Describe how you feel like now.

Veronica: It's hard to describe. I'm just floating. I AM (*with a big tear running down her cheek*).

P: Is there anything or anyone around you?

Veronica: No, I'm just here.

P: Can you elaborate?

Veronica: The world as I know it is not here. I'm so at peace.

P: What are you aware of?

Veronica: That this is where I want to be, where I want to stay. This is where I really belong.

P: Is this is a good place to ask some questions about Veronica?

It may seem I ask her this question very early on in her session, but more than thirty minutes have passed getting her into this deep state of consciousness. Between each question I ask and each answer I get from her quite some time passes, as she responds very slowly and deliberately. A past-life and life-between-life session can last over three hours.

Veronica: Yes.

P: Veronica describes how she doesn't belong, how she struggles to fit in.

Veronica: Being here now I understand.

P: Please help me understand.

Veronica: Deep down inside she remembers this state. She's longing to go back here.

P: I see. What would you advise?

Veronica: She needs to attune to this place.

P: Why hasn't she?

Veronica: She had forgotten.

P: You say, 'she's longing to go back here'.

Veronica: Yes, that's why she has been feeling so alienated with everything and everybody around her.

P: What are you suggesting?

Veronica: It's not that she needs to leave this earth.

P: Please explain.

Veronica: Before she wanted to leave. She wanted to be connected to something more meaningful.

P: And now she won't?

Veronica: It's not about leaving the world. It's about bringing this consciousness down into the human experience.

P: Please go on.

Veronica: When we are not connected we want to escape the earthly reality. We think transcendental awareness is the answer. But even this is a limited way of looking at things.

P: How so?

Veronica: Real awakening is when you are here on earth, yet awakened to the transcendental consciousness.

P: So there is no need to 'escape'?

Veronica: Exactly. The idea of escaping is a narrow way of looking at things. Rather it's about integrating.

P: You mean integrating the transcendental into day-to-day awareness?

Veronica: Yes, Veronica needs to stop trying to escape, thinking that elsewhere it is going to be better.

P: What do you suggest instead?

Veronica: I'm feeling so free and alive right now. There is no world. There is no reason why Veronica can't feel this way too.

P: Yes, because you are Veronica too?

Veronica: Yes, yes that's it.

P: There's no two 'yous'.

Veronica: Veronica separates in her mind the higher world from the reality of her day-to-day consciousness. But they can co-exist.

P: That's a high concept.

Veronica: It's the goal. What use it is to have to leave this place to descend to earth and remain stuck in a normal state of mind. Unless you bring the light down with you there will always be the divide.

P: The divide in consciousness?

Veronica: Yes, the divide between thinking that you can't experience bliss and freedom while you are attached to the body.

P: You think Veronica will remember?

Veronica: Once you have been here you can't go back. Now you know.

P: How do you suggest Veronica integrates this experience?

Veronica: Meditate.

P: Can you elaborate?

Veronica: Meditation on this experience, on this state I'm in right now, will allow her to reconnect. Through practice, she can bring down this experience and integrate it into her consciousness.

P: That is huge.

Veronica: She has felt alienated because she didn't realize that she can open up to this superconscious state and invite it in. She thought she instead needed to leave this world.

P: How does this realization make you feel?

Veronica: Amazing. Please allow me some time alone.

I leave her alone for a while and ask her to let me know when she is done.

Veronica: Ok, I'm done.

P: How are you feeling?

Veronica: Good.

P: Just good?

Veronica: Beyond good (*A smile*).

P: Veronica wrote down a list of questions. You want

me to read out some of them?

Veronica: You can, but they're of no consequence.

P: They're not?

Veronica: No.

P: Why not?

Veronica: These are questions that arise out of the fear and limited consciousness of Veronica

P: Wouldn't you want to answer them for the sake of Veronica?

Veronica: I am Veronica too. She will remember.

She is now integrating her experience of higher consciousness with Veronica. She realizes there is no separation between the two sides of her. She understands that Veronica and her higher consciousness is one and the same, just looking at it from a different angle.

P: Ok, so no need for any further questions?

Veronica: No, not really. I got it.

P: How would you summarize your experience today?

Veronica: I got what I needed most. To remember who I am and what state I'm capable of.

P: How will this help you as Veronica henceforth?

Veronica: Now I remember I have a place to go back to. And I need to open myself to allow this consciousness to permeate every aspect of my life. It's not about leaving. It's about living the right way. Unless I bring this higher consciousness back in my life as Veronica I don't really live to the fullness of my potential.

P: Well said.

Veronica: It's about living to the fullest.

P: Yes, the enlightened life.

Veronica: The higher consciousness is what lights up everyday experiences. I'm only as lonely and disconnected to others to the extent I haven't allowed the light to shine through my consciousness.

P: So you need to integrate.

Veronica: Yes.

P: Is there anything we may have missed today?

Veronica: No, I'm satisfied.

It is easy to disregard the significance of this session. When you meet clients who travel back in time through lives as kings, paupers, prisoners, hunters or temple priestesses, one tends to not get excited about these more abstract journeys. Meeting a client who experiences no such journeys, and who instead enters a formless, visionless and eventless state of consciousness can easily be misunderstood or disregarded unless you yourself understand what this state is about.

Even the way we regard the afterlife is a projection of our own subconscious expectations. We secretly hope and expect this afterlife to be an extension of life here on earth, but then only with the positive aspects of life. We hope it to be a world of comfort and beauty minus the hatefulness and negativity we encounter on earth.

But if we look at super consciousness, turiya, as a state that is beyond duality, we realize that expecting the afterlife to be just a world of positives minus negatives isn't realistic. Plus can only exist with minus. You can't have just one without the other. Instead, it makes more sense to regard it as a dimension that transcends life as we know it.

So how do we reconcile the experience of souls who do experience the afterlife as a beautiful organized world, with other souls who experience it as a formless state of consciousness beyond the duality of the world?

The experiences are both true. These depend on the impressions the soul brings along when it passes on. The astral body is the accumulation of impressions gathered during many lives and is wrapped around the soul like a sheath. Even after death, we project our reality through that sheath. We see it through the filter of our previous experiences.

Since most of us are pretty earthbound when we die, we carry a strong sense of conditioning with us even when we die. And so the earth-like idea of heaven is carried forward to the in-between-life state.

Does this mean that the experience isn't really true then? It is true, to the same degree our life here is true. How true is our earthly experience really? We see, hear, feel and smell a reality that is shaped by the range of our senses. Imagine what it would be like if you didn't have these senses. Would you still experience the same reality? If your senses were a thousand times stronger or your eyes were as powerful as the most powerful microscope on earth what kind of reality would you perceive? Most probably you wouldn't experience matter as we know it. You would see only energy.

The astral body too is like an instrument with senses. It contains the totality of our memories and impressions. Just like we experience earth through the body and its senses, we see the afterlife through the astral senses and impressions as well. It's just subtler. Sometimes it is even possible to step out of the astral body and see reality beyond this sheath of conditioning.

The turiya state is that reality that is perceived when the soul momentarily transcends the conditioning of both bodily and astral senses, memories and impressions. Veronica connected to this state beyond conditioning, into pure awareness.

More importantly, she realized that this state is not just 'out there'. It can be experienced here on earth too. This section of this book is an introduction to this concept. The three pillars of life are sub-purposes to this larger realization. Veronica, having her basic needs met and her life pretty much in order, now moved on to her highest soul's purpose, the awakening to higher consciousness while in the body, here and now.

Veronica's case and the following cases in these chapters are all variants of how this highest consciousness can be experienced, both in a state after death, but also while still in the body here on earth.

Chapter 13
Beyond The Waves Of The Mind

You were walking at night and you didn't see that workers had removed the wall around the old medieval well, because it had fallen into disrepair. The well was completely exposed and the old stones that formed the wall around it were piled up on one side. Due to the darkness, you didn't see the cones and warning signs and you fell all the way down thirty feet deep into the water.

Shocked and completely drenched, you're glad you're alive and that the water in the well protected your fall.

Trying to orient yourself and recovering from the shock, you try to scale the walls to get out. But to no avail. It's too slippery. Fortunately, there is some dry sand around the water and you drag yourself onto it. Not able to see a way out you start to panic.

Screaming, shouting, you beat the walls but to no avail. Nobody can hear you, you are too deep down. You become increasingly frantic, shouting louder till your voice hurts and then fails. After thirty minutes of grasping and shouting you collapse down in desperation, now thoroughly depressed at the thought of dying here alone. Weeping for a long time and completely exhausted you realize there is nobody to save you. This realization makes your blood boil. You beat the walls even harder, cursing out God and everything that lives. "How can this happen. What is this, why is this happening to me? It's all your fault. How could you allow this to happen?" Still nothing, nobody there to help. God doesn't show up to lift you out.

After exhausting all your emotions, you fall into silence. Calm now because you simply don't have any energy left. You just sit there, staring aimlessly. When you calm down and your emotions evaporate, you start to see things clearer. To your amazement, you realize that all along, there in the corner, are metal steps anchored in the old wall. Steps that you can use to climb out of the well. You didn't see it because you were so wrapped up in emotions. Your panic, your depression, your anger, clouded your mind. No matter what emotion came up, no matter what you told yourself and made yourself believe, nothing changed. Neither the panic, nor the depression, nor the anger improved anything in your situation. It is only when you calmed down that the fog of emotions in your head lifted and you actually started to investigate the well. You were too preoccupied with emotions earlier. The stories you told yourself are what flashed before your eyes, not a clear picture of the walls of the well.

It didn't matter why you fell into the well. It also didn't matter what you felt in the well and what kind of emotions, opinion, and thoughts clouded your mind. You were still in the well and nothing changed that reality.

This is the story of our lives. People who believe that merely environmental conditions, parental influence, and genetic predisposition are responsible for their current reality tend to think, deep down, that they are not responsible. They are simply born this way and in these circumstances. They believe they have no choice in this. People that are born privileged consider themselves superior and fortunate and people that have been born in difficult circumstances feel weak and powerless. But we can all fall into the well. We don't know when karma will catch up with us.

Whatever deck of cards you may have been dealt, you alone are responsible to work with what you have been given. No matter how you got here, or what your belief system is, this is what you have to work with. You may complain all you want and defer the responsibility. If you want to change, nobody is going to do it for you. Nobody is going to get you out of that well. The quicker you wake up to that reality, the better it is for you.

What stands in the way of seeing what is possible, and what the way out is, are the waves of emotions that arise in our mind. These come partially from the outside world and partially from the inside of our mind. It so happens that the definition of yoga, according to the ancient philosopher Patañjali, talks about these mind waves. It goes as follows;

Yogah chitta vritti nirodhah. This is Sanskrit and translates as 'yoga is the cessation of the waves of the mind'.

Cessation here means a ceasing, a stopping of the waves of the mind. The word yoga means union (derived from the Sanskrit the word 'yuj' means 'to unite or integrate'). Let me explain this idea of union by giving you a short metaphorical story.

Begin to visualize a large lake high up in the mountains. It's a sunny day but the wind is blowing viciously and it is creating large ripples and waves. These waves, in turn, stir up debris from the bottom of the lake. If you are swimming underwater this murky rubble clouds your vision. The rubble and these waves prevent you from even seeing the sun shining above the surface.

If you are swimming in the lake and the storm suddenly stops, you see the waves subside and the rubble sinking back down to the bottom. Within minutes the water becomes completely clear and the surface of the lake smooth like a mirror.

Diving beneath the surface again you now see the beautiful rays of the sun piercing through the crystal clear water creating an amazing spectacle.

During and after the wind storm the sun was always shining. But under the rough waters, you couldn't see anything. When the waves of the mind subside, we can see the sun of our higher Self shine through the mind.

The conscious mind is the surface of the lake where the storm of never-ending thoughts rages. The subconscious mind is the underwater world where rubble is stirred up by this storm.

In Christianity, we say 'the kingdom of God is within'. In eastern philosophy, we say 'we are the soul'. As Pierre Teilhard de Chardin said: 'We are spirits having a human experience, not human beings having a spiritual experience'.

Compare our essence, our higher Self, to the sun. It is always shining, irrespective of the waves in your mind. I may not feel this inner light because my mind and my subconscious is like that stormy lake. There's always stuff going on, storms raging, rubble and dirt floating around. Only when it calms down is the sun able to shine through the lake. When that happens we start to taste the internal light and peace, coming from within. When you are able to calm down the waves of your mind, you start to experience this peace.

Union or true yoga happens when your higher Self connects with the ultimate reality, unobstructed by the waves of your mind.

In this state of complete connectedness, we can draw health, prosperity, and energy into our lives. This is not a religious concept. This is the science of the mind. The conscious and subconscious mind needs to become calm, clear and transparent, so that union, yoga, can happen.

When the waves of the mind subside, we start to reach into the deeper, calmer recesses of our true Self. We exist at three levels, the body, the mind and underneath those there exists the higher Self. This higher Self is the light which illumines all these different layers.

THE NATURE OF WAVES

The nature of these waves is desires. That is what the Buddhist philosophy states as the cause of suffering. But what can we do with these desires? We hear from the pulpits that we need to renounce desires. But how do you do that? And should we really? I myself tried this via my twenty-one years I spent as a monk in a monastery. Everything was driven by this effort to renounce and overcome these desires.

I have second thoughts about this method now. When I meet a client and I see that this client has a certain strong desire in life, even when I clearly see that this person would be better off not having that desire, the desire is not going to go away because of my advice.

It seems to me now that when we try to remove the waves of the mind, instead of advising somebody to 'renounce' this desire, or advise this person to try to 'overcome' this desire, there are more effective approaches available.

The first method is simple. Help this person fulfill this desire. This can be a difficult task, especially when this person at this point in time does not have the capacity to fulfill the desire. Like wanting to be wealthy without having the required education or experience. What causes suffering is having a desire that cannot yet be fulfilled. This causes restless waves in the mind.

Instead of telling that person to be realistic and renounce this desire that is standing in the way of peace of mind, it seems better to show that person how to get educated and prepared and gain the required qualifications to make the kind of money he desires. When this capacity has been achieved, he can experience for himself what it feels like to make money. Only then will he be a fair judge as to whether this money will bring him the happiness and peace he is looking for. We need the experience first.

Another way to deal with desires, once the experience has been gained and a person is mentally and spiritually sufficiently matured, is to enlighten his consciousness. Help that person understand that what he earlier desired was something not really conducive to happiness. It is not really a renouncing, but a spiritual becoming aware, a maturing. Like when we are middle-aged we suddenly realize that the childish desires we had as a kid are not really what we desire today. We are now more enlightened, more grown-up and can let go. We have not renounced these desires but have outgrown them. We have become sufficiently wise to see that those earlier fancies are silly and useless to us now.

In a life-between-life session, your higher Self and spiritual guides generally advise the soul depending on the above two scenarios. If the soul still needs to experience certain things, they advise it to go ahead and gain the required experiences. But if the soul already has been experiencing certain things over and over again and still keeps on repeating the same patterns, they may intervene and encourage a soul to make the change and give up the habit and desire.

The long term goal is to silence the desires and waves in the mind. In order to achieve an awakened consciousness, these waves have to be subdued. Awakened consciousness is a mind without desires for themselves. Such a soul lives for the wellbeing of others. The waves in the subconscious and conscious mind have ceased. Such a mind is quiet and clear. As a result, the light and consciousness of the inner Self are shining brightly from within. Such a soul is able to commune with a higher consciousness beyond. The individual Self is in unison with the cosmic Self, with the Source.

A COSMIC EXPERIENCE

Once in a while, I have a client who, during a life-between-lives regression session, gets in direct contact with the Source. This source is beyond even the life-between-life dimension. There have been several encounters where a client was completely absorbed in ecstatic divine energy. These are very intense and transformative experiences and are rare and precious. I've had clients curl up in their chair in such bliss that they were crying out loudly. I don't want to create a false image by making you think that every client will have such an incredible experience, because indeed it is rare. I do want to share with you such a case though for the simple reason that this can happen and that it possible for some of us to reach such tremendous spiritual heights during a session.

The following case is of a 34-year-old woman from Southern California named Cheryl. At the time of this session, I still separated the past-life regression session from the life-between-life regression session and took two days for this process. Nowadays I do the past-life regression and the life-between-life regression session in one day for the simple reason that it takes too much time and most clients can't afford to spend two days away from home. I've also found that doing the past-life and life-between-lives in one session allows for a more seamless flow. However, during Cheryl's session, I dedicated more time than usual to exploring past-lives and I could take her back to several past lives before entering the life between-life dimension.

Cheryl's past was very interesting. In her last life, she was a young twenty-four-year-old American army scout named sergeant Tom who was shot in the back behind enemy lines in Europe during World War II. Cheryl told me afterward that even today she still bears the scar on her back from the shot that killed her. In another lifetime she was a temple priest in India who spent his entire life performing ritualistic worships. In yet another life she was an itinerant woman ascetic in the Himalayas who drowned in a flood.

When I helped her cross over to the life-between-lives world the first stop was an orientation. Orientation is where the soul looks back over its past lives and reflects on what it has learned. In Cheryl's case, there was no guide and her higher Self spoke lucidly about her past lives.

P: What do you remember most from your last moments as Sergeant Tom?

Cheryl: I remember as I was dying thinking about my little sister and how much I loved her. I was worried about how she would continue on without me.

P: What happened next?

Cheryl: I recall seeing my body lying on the ground face down. My buddy was trying to get to me but we were under heavy fire. He was screaming 'Are you ok?' But I was already out of my body. I remember feeling as if I was floating up slowly towards the sky.

I was not afraid. Instead, I felt very at peace. It was like a relief.

P: What else did you observe?

Cheryl: It was intense. It was like all emotions happening at once, yet I felt completely detached from them. As if the energy from this traumatic experience was resonating around me, but I was already on my way out.

P: Continue.

Cheryl: I felt a tremendous pull in my heart to go towards the light. As if my mind and heart fused as one entity. Completely free.

P: How do you relate to sergeant Tom?

Cheryl: I feel a tremendous amount of love for Tom. He was a really loving, selfless and kindhearted person. I feel proud to have lived this life as him, even though it was short. It made me realize that no matter what kind of life you live, each life is filled with amazing moments.

P: Can you give an example?

Cheryl: When we realize that we are not just one body, that we experience many different lives, and that each one of them has lessons and experiences of love, pain, loss and all kinds of emotions, there is a freedom that comes from the realization that I am the spirit that travels what seems timelessly through these different lives. Each life is a gift, and each experience is an opportunity to feel something.

P: What did you learn as Sergeant Tom?

Cheryl: I learned the value of brotherhood and to not be afraid to die. I learned that life itself, to be alive, regardless of the circumstances, is amazing. Even the moment before my death, when I took my last breath, was incredible.

I now know that all the qualities that made sergeant Tom so special are still with me. That brings a sense of comfort, almost as if I am not alone.

P: How does this relate to your earlier life as an Indian temple priest?

Cheryl: It doesn't relate. It was a different kind of life with a different kind of purpose.

P: Please help me understand.

Cheryl: In my life as a priest I devoted my entire self to God. I was fortunate enough to be able to sit in meditation and have access to incredible spiritual knowledge and wisdom.

P: What was this experience like?

Cheryl: I was the head priest in a small village in India. My main duty was to tend to the deities in the temple. People would come to receive blessings and for me to perform worships and specific rituals. I felt extremely blessed in this life.

P: What was the most essential realization in this life and how does it manifest in Cheryl's life?

Cheryl: I picked this life to build up my spiritual energy and to rest my soul. I can see how this life has influenced Cheryl because she has this unique ability to stay calm and centered in her own energy. She also has a deep love for God.

However, Cheryl feels the need to engage more deeply with people in her relationships than the temple priest did. He kept to himself too much.

P: In what way?

Cheryl: He lived alone most of his life and did not engage in the activities of the community and family.

His life was not complete. It felt one-sided. Deep down inside he had a longing to connect more deeply with people. He was only living a spiritual life, but not a human life. Cheryl is trying to balance both these lives.

P: How do you feel right now?

Cheryl: I'm feeling very light and peaceful.

P: The spirit world is wide open to you. Is there any place you would like to visit?

Cheryl: No, I'm already here.

P: Where is here?

Cheryl: Home is right here, where I am now.

P: Can you share what home feels like?

Cheryl: (*ecstatic*) I feel myself as a black hole. A tremendous amount of energy. This is feminine divine energy. All my experiences are Hers. As if this black hole's consciousness is dreaming up this reality. It's a feeling of being at a center point, yet everything around me is me as well.

P: A sense of infinity?

Cheryl: I feel myself as infinite space. As if my consciousness is the creator itself. And my own voice is the voice of God.

It's overwhelming (*even more ecstatic*). My human body and brain cannot even begin to conceive my true nature.

P: How do you define that true nature?

Cheryl: All I can say is that it is such an immense

feeling of love and that there is no other feeling than love. Love is just a word we use to try and describe the temporary experience of being connected to our true nature.

But imagine, if that temporary experience of love was continually expanding out in all directions infinitely, with a power that no human could ever comprehend.

P: Then what happens?

Cheryl: I feel I'm being consumed. I feel myself completely as Her.

Cheryl is crying out in joy. She is curled up in her chair weeping profoundly. She stays in this state for the next few minutes. She can't speak. She is clearly expressing signs of divine ecstasy. I'm looking at this in amazement and feel the energy in the room expanding. I'm in the presence of divine energy and its overwhelming, as if a portal to another dimension has opened up. It is hard not to get overwhelmed by this myself. When after a few minutes she still doesn't come out of the experience I slowly check in trying to get her to come back again. It took a while to reconnect with her. It was like trying to get somebody to wake up from anesthesia. She was in a completely different state of consciousness. Her eyes had rolled up in her sockets and where white.

P: How are you feeling now?

Cheryl: It's impossible to express in words.

P: If you could, how would you express it.

Cheryl: It's like dissolving in an ocean of bliss.

I noticed that she had a hard time speaking and she didn't feel like saying much more. The experience was still lingering and I let her come down slowly. After a while, we ended the session. I will never forget this incredible soul's experience. It was an important understanding for me as a life-between-life therapist to see what is possible when you work with a highly advanced soul. I was fortunate enough to get a glimpse of infinity through her amazing experience.

When we read accounts of life-between-lives regression sessions, we usually regard the life-between-life world as an earth-like extension of our life here on this planet. In my experience, this is just one way of looking at the afterlife. Throughout this book, I am sharing the idea that there are many different levels of consciousness the soul can ascend to when leaving the physical world.

Cheryl's case is a beautiful example of such an ascended consciousness. Though at first, she enters the life-between-life dimension as we traditionally know it, she then ascends to a much higher frequency.

Some quantum physicists have accepted consciousness as the substratum of our universe. They argue, that when we regard our world as not material but energetic, it must still be resting on something. Energy must still be somewhere. They speculate that this something, this somewhere, is consciousness. This school of mystical quantum physics has much in common with the experiences of my life-between-life clients. The higher the soul ascends, the more it identifies with the underlying Source energy of the universe. And from the experiences of clients in this state, this Source seems to be divine in nature. An infinite ocean of celestial and blissful consciousness.

Theoretically, we can all ascend into this consciousness, considering that this is our true nature. Nothing else really exists. We see and experience diversity because we are still identified with our individual consciousness. The collective memories of our experiences over many lifetimes are wrapped around the soul like an energetic sheath. We look at life, even the afterlife, through this veil and see a representation of it, like looking through a filter.

When we are still earthbound, just after passing on from the physical world, this strong identification with the body and the life we just lived makes us experience an earth-like afterlife when we pass on. But then, gradually, as we disassociate more from the body and our life here on earth, the soul can start to ascend into higher levels of consciousness.

We don't have to die for this. Our belief system is responsible for our range of perception.

What I mean by this, is that when we accept that there is another dimension, we can, at first in our imagination, travel there. The more you imagine and the more you make this imagination come alive, the easier your consciousness can reach there. This belief, this acceptance, makes you in a way less earthbound. You become more open.

The more sensitive we become, the more we can pick up. Highly intuitive souls pick up much more information than ordinary people. So if we want to expand, reach out into higher consciousness, we need to learn how to detach from our Earth-like density.

The general concept is as follows, the more we believe that this earth is all that exists, the more earthbound we will be. We won't be open to connecting with something that could possibly exist beyond the range of our senses. How could we, because in our mind it doesn't exist. I don't see or feel it, therefore it doesn't exist. Science has long upheld this belief, for the simple reason that it wasn't yet capable of observing a world beyond matter.

This same science has now helped us see that what we perceive with our senses isn't accurate at all. With the emergence of quantum physics, we now know that matter doesn't exist as we know it and that our mind, and the world we perceive with it, is a mere interpreter of reality.

Our mind stands between actual reality and what we experience as our reality. It creates a distorted image based on its limited senses. The key is to work with the mind. As our mind becomes clearer, purer, and calmer, so will our perception of reality.

Yogis, therefore, have traditionally made their primary focus on the mind. Clear the mind in order to perceive a higher and more accurate perception of reality. The mind is our reality. That's why it is so hard to convince certain people of your political views. In our minds, it is incomprehensible that some people can be so stupid. How can you possibly vote for this guy and believe these things? Can't you see that you are being deceived? No, they can't see. This is the reality in their minds. This is the world they perceive. There isn't just one world. Everybody's world is completely different. We all live on what seems to be a different planet. Consider this. Your world is completely false too. There is no material world, technically. All that exists is energy that moves in consciousness.

I realize that this seems to be taking it a bit far. Yet it is the truth. The question is, how can this help me where I am now? The first thing to consider is that I can shape my reality with my own mind. I can improve my individual consciousness and accordingly my own world. If enough people think this way we can shape our own collective reality.

As my mind changes, so does my world. If I want to experience a higher consciousness here and now, I need to first tune into it with my mind. Think of the famous medium Tyler Henry. What is his reality like? He lives in two realities at once. He is here with you and me, and he is communing with the minds of souls that have passed on to the life-between-life dimension. For him, the world that you and I see is just one aspect of reality. He knows from personal experience that there is much more than meets the eye.

I have personally lived with such visionary souls. And I still know souls that are elevated in this way. Their consciousness lives partially here with us on this earth, and it is partially beyond. They can reach into it, commune with it, travel there and derive inspiration, strength, and energy from it. They all have one characteristic in common, that they live with an unbounded sense of freedom and joy.

We are much freer than we realize. When we learn how to calm down the waves in our mind, when the impermanent projection of our past memories subsides, we can start to experience a reality that is vast and brilliant. This is our birthright; this is our destiny. When the light of higher consciousness shines in our hearts and minds we can experience a tremendous amount of happiness and peace. This can be experienced here and now.

Chapter 14
Understanding The Nature Of Duality

Once in a while, I meet a client who is highly philosophical by nature. It is always interesting to me, seeing a client walk into my office, to discover what kind of personality and temperament I'm dealing with. A common question a lot of people have is: "What if I can't be hypnotized?" To that, I reply: "Don't worry, because the internal state we're trying to reach is natural to you. Every night when you fall asleep you pass through the Theta state; the same state we use for a life-between-lives regression. When you fall asleep, you drop down from your awake Beta state, then through the Alpha and Theta states to end up in Delta, sleep. It's not that we magically need to create a mind wave that is totally unknown to you. If that would be the case each life-between-life session would be a complete gamble, because we wouldn't know if you could enter a previously unknown and mysterious realm. Fortunately, we are able, due to the techniques we use, to hold one for prolonged periods of time in the Theta state, a state that one normally passes through quickly in the process of falling asleep."

Each client, when in the Theta state, communicates with me differently. Some express things more visually, some more kinesthetically and some more mentally. The visual person will see more literal and graphic representations of a supernatural world, whereas a mental person tends to experience this state in a more abstract way. A kinesthetic temperament will be feeling things more. Each client experience is as intense as the other, just in different ways. I never try to qualify or prefer one over the other, as each experience is unique and interesting in its own way.

Joey was such a mental person. Quiet and delicate, he seemed a sensitive and philosophical kind of guy. He was well versed in different schools of Eastern philosophy, was practicing meditation which showed in his life-between-lives session. My observation of him soon turned out to be correct. His session will always go down memory lane as an unforgettable one. It turned out he wasn't much for visuals, but he was hyper-suggestible, meaning he entered the hypnotic state rapidly and deeply.

As a footnote, the ease of induction isn't necessarily a sign that we will have a better session, just that the theta state is accessed quickly. Some people simply need more time, and this is why at the start of each session I always take a lot of time making clients feel safe and secure so that each individual can enter the Theta state at his or her own pace. Once people feel secure and comfortable they will eventually trust the situation enough to let go and relax and end up having a wonderful session. Creating such an environment isn't merely a therapeutic technique, but it is also something that a therapist needs to cultivate and share as an extension of his or her own inner state of being. This can't be taught, it's a skill that comes through experience and inner growth.

Joey's past life regression was uneventful and I don't need to spend much time on it in this chapter. He described life as a hunter somewhere in the mountains of the Americas. Looking out over vast mountain ranges in the snow, with his faithful dog at his side. A peaceful existence, reflecting on the meaning of life and happy and content with being alone and having what he called true freedom.

When we moved into the life-between-life realm, he entered a unique state where he wasn't really seeing or experiencing a sense of an afterlife world, but more a sense of becoming connected to a superconscious state beyond any shapes or forms. The ensuing conversation is dear to my heart as it has much in common with Eastern and Vedic philosophy, a subject I studied deeply for many years. So, fortunately, I was able to keep up with him in this very unique case. The transcript of his audio file goes as follows:

P: What do you notice?

J: I'm not noticing a particular thing. It's a state of being.

P: Can you explain this to me?

J: I just AM.

P: Are there any guides nearby, or can you discern any kind of presence?

J: No, there are no guides.

P: So you are alone in this state?

J: Alone is not the right way to describe this. I'm part of a whole.

P: Tell me more.

J: I am conscious that I am, yet I am part of something larger. An infinite space that has no boundaries.

P: Can you see this?

J: In a way yes. It's light everywhere and I am light. It's a knowing, a connectedness.

P: So there are no forms and shapes here?

J: No. Just light.

P: What does this light feel like?

J: A sense of infinity. And freedom.

P: Freedom from what?

J: Limitations.

P: What kind of limitations?

J: The kind we experience on earth.

P: Is Joey experiencing these kinds of limitations?

J: Yes, of course.

P: Why of course? Is everybody feeling this?

J: It's the nature of our world.

P: What do you mean?

J: The nature of our world is duality.

P: What does that mean exactly, duality?

J: The pairs of opposites, light and dark, good and evil, warm and cold. These coexist. Always.

P: You say always?

J: On earth, in a normal conscious state of mind yes, always.

P: Interesting that you say 'normal state of mind'. Are you implying that it is possible to not be subjected to duality when you're not in an 'ordinary' state of mind?

J: Yes, like I am now. My body is here on earth but my awareness is in a way beyond the pairs of opposites.

P: Can you explain what these pairs of opposites really mean in practical terms. I mean, we say for example that God is good. Good is the opposite of bad. So God would be subject to the pairs of opposites?

J: Saying that God is good is limiting Gods true nature. God is beyond good and bad. Beyond the pairs of opposites, beyond the nature of duality.

P: So you're saying that when we say God's nature is good that's incorrect?

J: If you look at God as a man sitting in some heavenly sphere looking down on us then yes, that is a very restricted view of reality. In my experience, God is an infinite reality, an expanse of consciousness.

P: But people have seen Jesus and Buddha. Isn't that God having a human form?

J: Both are true.

P: Correct me if I'm wrong, but doesn't this sound like a contradiction? First, you say that God is beyond good and evil, and yet here you say he can appear as having a human form on earth.

J: It depends on the state of mind of the observer. If you are in a normal state of mind you will see God as a human being. But if you ascend beyond duality, God loses form and will be experienced as infinity beyond name and form.

P: So you are saying that when we experience God as a human being then we superimpose human qualities like good and evil on his form?

J: Like you are doing now, calling God a man.

P: (*laughing*) Yes, correct. I read somewhere an analogy about water and ice. Both are water, but one is frozen and has become solid. Similarly, the true nature of ice is water, even though we can experience it as having a definite form and shape.

J: Yes.

P: Like a wave and the ocean. A wave has form but loses it once it merges back with the ocean. Something like that?

J: Yes.

P: Is it wrong to say God is good?

J: No, not at all. But it causes us to wonder why there is evil. Instead, we can look at creation as one living and breathing entity, one where good and evil are but two sides of the same coin.

P: You mean that good and evil and all pairs of opposites belong together?

J: Yes, part of the same creation. You can't have good without evil like you can't have light without darkness. There is no freedom from evil as long as you are subject to the forces of nature. Evil, like goodness, are qualities of nature.

P: Hence the need to transcend?

J: Yes, freedom from pain is the transcendence of both good and evil.

P: How do you do that? I mean, yes, I want to be free from pain and worry, but I don't necessarily want to leave this world.

J: I don't mean physically leaving this world.

P: You mean in your mind?

J: It is possible to cultivate a state of consciousness that is so elevated that you are not subject to the ups and downs of this world. Your body will always be subjected to it, as it is part of this world, and even your mind will be to some extent. But there is a state of being that transcends body and mind.

P: I understand this from a philosophical standpoint, but isn't this too much for most people?

J: Even understanding this intellectually can be of great help.

P: How so?

J: When you understand that peace is found beyond the duality of this world, then you stop seeking it there. You will know that seeking wordily pleasure won't give you eternal happiness, because these pleasures are part of the finite world of duality. Eternal peace in infinity cannot exist in a finite world of duality. Every action has a reaction, equal and opposite. So pleasure will somehow cause a reaction.

P: Like having to work day and night to afford this pleasure.

J: Yes. Desires take you away from peace.

P: That begs the question, how do we transcend?

J: Through meditation, prayer, being more aware and having discernment.

P: The great non-dualist sage Ramana Maharshi said this too: "Find out who you really are. Ask yourself: Who am I?" Jesus said: "The Kingdom of God is within," which to me means God is not in the world but in a higher state of consciousness.

J: The soul is not affected by duality. Only the body and the mind is.

P: So we need to transcend body and mind consciousness and connect to our Soul Self?

J: Yes.

P: How is Joey doing in this regard?

J: He understands the concept and had some glimpses of this state in meditation. But he still craves some of the distractions of the world.

P: What do you suggest he do?

J: Most of his indulgences are the result of bad habits and laziness. He already knows this is not helping him. He needs to be stronger.

P: Can you be more specific, for his sake?

J: It's a choice he needs to make. Nothing is good or bad in itself. The choices he makes result in a certain outcome. If he keeps having bad habits his mind will suffer the results of these bad choices. If, on the other hand, he chooses to meditate more regularly and keep his mind clean, it will be so much easier for him to lift his mind.

P: Action-reaction.

J: Yes, we all have a choice. Nobody is forcing us to do anything. Only our mind does. That's why you want to cultivate good habits.

P: Are you implying that bad habits make us do things we don't really want to do?

J: The mind can work for you or against you. So cultivate good habits.

P: I like to get back to how this is going to be practical for Joey and his daily problems.

J: You're confusing comfortable with practical. It may not be comfortable for him to change his habits, but it is very practical.

P: How so?

J: Anytime you try to change a habit it is uncomfortable. But it is very practical to change ones' habits so that the karmas of these habits don't keep bothering you.

P: Short-term enjoyment versus long-term benefit?

J: He has a hard time keeping his mind elevated because he has to spend too much energy in dealing with the results of his bad decisions. This is a karmic pattern. Once he becomes more aware and changes this vicious cycle his mind will become free.

P: You mean he won't be so much bothered by the results of his bad actions and he will have energy left to dedicate to meditation? And this will result in a happier state of mind?

J: Yes, he needs to cultivate a meditation habit. The practical outcome will be peace and balance.

P: I'm still struggling to see the practical side, the day to day benefit, in this for Joey. How to strive for a transcendental consciousness above the duality of this world? Doesn't that take the joy out of living?

J: You don't strive for a transcendental consciousness.

P: You don't?

J: It happens when you start to understand. When Joey becomes more aware, he will start making better choices. This will eventually help him transcend.

P: What about enjoying one's life?

J: You don't really enjoy life until you attain higher consciousness.

P: Please help me understand because I have a feeling that many will disagree.

J: A mind pulled down in the senses isn't really enjoying life at its fullest. A mind that is pure and enlightened enjoys life so much more.

P: Like looking at life through a dirty lens versus looking at it through a clean lens?

J: Yes. Nobody says you shouldn't enjoy life. You should, but you have to know how. Enjoying life elevated means you live in a way that lifts you up, instead of one that takes you down.

P: Summarizing what you just said, when you learn how to enjoy properly you feel better and you improve your future. Because by being aware of the consequences of your actions you don't create new karmic bondages that you will have to face in the future. Instead, you work towards inner freedom. And this inner freedom will eventually help you slowly transcend the duality of this world?

J: Yes.

I love this case for several reasons:

1: This is a client who is already well informed about certain philosophical issues before he enters the session. This allows him to clearly articulate certain difficult issues. The result is a conversation about the nature of our world that is precious.

2: He is able to make an abstract philosophic concept, namely the duality of this world, understandable.

3: He is able to make this concept practical for his normal self, Joey.

4: He encourages both the attainment of Higher Consciousness while helping us understand that it doesn't need to happen at the expense of enjoying life here on earth. I find this to be a very important point because it allows us to truly integrate living a spiritual life with living a worldly life.

This last point is an issue that I have found to be very confusing for many seekers. Look back at the history of Christianity for example. Isn't it true that enjoying life has always been equated with being sinful? I'm not talking about some of the modern-day American preachers who preach a gospel of wealth (for themselves mostly).

What I mean is that we have been burdened by guilt when we think of enjoying life. As a result, many people have simply rejected religion to plunge into a life without any thought for tomorrow. I used to see this tendency in

India too where I was part of a religious tradition. We were continuously encouraged to 'renounce' the world. The trouble with this kind of thinking is that if you are not careful you will throw out the joy of living along with renouncing its bondage.

Joey's case gives us an insight into how we can live a happy life in the world while working towards an ascended superconscious state of inner freedom. I've always held the belief, and have been sharing this with my clients, that it is important to have a philosophy of life. Something you can hold on to in times of trouble, but more so a true North that holds you on course. A guiding principle by which you can measure all your decisions. Once you know your target coordinates, all you have to do is set your GPS and it will guide you there. Without these coordinates, on what do you base your life's decisions? You don't have a frame of reference. So it's not, when we want to live a truly spiritual life, that we can't enjoy life, but more that the decisions we make need to be in line with our end destination. If enjoyment is part of that journey, then we can enjoy fully. If the enjoyment takes us away from that goal, then it will be detrimental for us in the long run.

Renouncing to me now, after all these years, means letting go, willingly and consciously, of those distractions that may at first seem tempting, but that ends up making me feel miserable later. It's like eating a greasy and fatty meal. Every time I give in to this kind of craving I end up regretting it an hour later, feeling stuffed and bloated. Instead, I'm learning that there is a joy in being aware of what I eat because it keeps me sharp and light, a feeling that I value greatly. And this is important to me in a larger context, as I need to feel light and sharp if I want to keep my mind on the right path towards my life's ultimate goal. And so it is with all the things I do. I don't want to slip in some unconscious fog where I forget why I am here in the first place. I have found there to be a great inner joy unfolding when I live this way. Few things are bad in and of themselves. Things like money, love, and intimacy, these things are great if you know how to use them. These can be tools that help you uplift your life and that of others. These same things can become burdens and bring you down if you don't know how to handle them properly. What joy is life if you can't live it with your heart wide open? To protect this wide-open heart, however, we need a great deal of love, strength, and discernment. If we misunderstand or have a narrow and fearful view of spiritual life, there is a chance that will take the joy of life out of it. A true and free artist of life is one who is able to keep the mind pure and high while enjoying life to the fullest. These two are not mutually exclusive.

Once the waves of the mind are under control, joy emerges from within. You don't have to do much more at that point. It is just there. Perhaps that's why Joey in his higher conscious state said that you don't strive for a transcendent conscious state per se, but that it emerges by itself when you live in awareness. Just set your compass on this transcendental state, and then let go, keeping it just enough in your awareness to help you make the right decisions about the things that matter most in your life. That's the meaning of living in awareness. Aware of the end-target in the back of your mind allowing you to make the correct decisions now. This way you're never in darkness or confused.

An important reason people get depressed is that they never had, or have been disconnected from this greater goal. They feel lost and afraid. Or they just give up. They have identified themselves with one or many of the false masks they are wearing and don't see a reality beyond. These masks terrify them and they are even more afraid of what others think of them. They can't let go and look further. Without a clear life's vision, you have no direction and you can't make sense of what is happening around you or within you. You have a hard time making changes because you don't know in what direction that change needs to go, nor do you know how far you have strayed. And so people conform to the collective subconscious passively, willingly subjected to corporate and religious indoctrination.

Joy is primarily a state of mind that happens when we live our lives in accordance with divine principles. When we are in tune with ourselves and our life's goals a subtle joy becomes part of your daily experience. It's a joy that transcends the minor ups and downs life throws at us. And even when once in a while a large karmic wave hits our shores, we know how to hold on and let it pass.

I believe there are many levels of transcendental consciousness. You don't have to be enlightened to experience this. Becoming aware of your life's goals and trying to live accordingly is already a transcendental awareness. Because you transcend, philosophically, the limited notion that pure and sustaining joy can be found in the duality of this world. This provides great strength and prevents you from getting lost in it. Then as we progress we can slowly ascend into states of mind where joy is perpetually felt within. There is no end to how strong this inner joy can grow.

I mentioned living as a young man with a great Indian saint near Paris. Though enthusiastic and eager to live some kind of spiritual life, my immaturity and youth prevented me from feeling the peace I was longing for. When I asked the saint about it he looked at me smiling and said: "One day you will always feel strong and happy." At the time I found this hard to believe, knowing my own state of mind. But today, a few decades later, I actually feel a gentle inner peace and flow most of the time. I also see it getting stronger as I get older. It is the result of the decisions and adjustments I made earlier in life. So as long as we become aware of our ultimate goal and make the necessary adjustments, we will eventually arrive at a state of calm. It has to be so because our true nature is joy. Joy is the light of our own soul.

Chapter 15
The Wisdom Of The Awakened Ones

The following two cases are among the most extraordinary ones I have experienced. They bear testimony to the incredible spiritual awakening of two phenomenal women. They have made me more aware of the emergence of an awakening earth, as described in books like 'The Global Brain Awakens' (The Gaia hypothesis) by Peter Russells. If you were totally unfamiliar with the concept of spiritual awakening, you might be prone to discount the cases in this chapter as exaggerated or unrealistic. But for those familiar with the concept (and if you would have met such great souls yourself) you'd start to recognize patterns among an increasing amount of people having these incredible experiences. If I had only one such case amongst the hundreds of clients I have met, then I too may have doubted. But as you start witnessing more and more of these kinds of cases there is a realization that a global awakening is happening.

The first of these two cases revolve around a fifty-nine-year-old woman, a Ph.D. in Depth Psychology, who flew in from the Mid-West to meet me in my office in California. A tall, intelligent lady, with large and calm eyes, and a graceful demeanor.

Her past-life regression is one of the most amazing cases I have ever come across. She described a life where she was a gypsy-like free spirit who from an early age wandered alone in an internally awakened state of consciousness. I like to share with you most of the details of this case.

P: What are you wearing?

Catherine: I'm barefoot. I'm wearing a white long gown.

P: What's your age?

Catherine: I'm 14 years old.

P: Can you describe the area you are in right now?

Catherine: I'm looking at the trees. Big, tall pine trees. I'm in the forest. The light is filtering through. It seems I can push the trees back with my hands to see more.

P: Are you near a village, a town, or is it remote?

Catherine: Remote (*again, it is common for somebody in a deep state to respond in short terse answers, especially at the beginning of the session. They often speak very softly and slow at first*).

P: Is your house anywhere nearby?

Catherine: No house.

P: So you're here alone. What are you doing here at this moment?

Catherine: Just being. Walking.

P: How do you feel at this moment?

Catherine: Confident. Light.

P: So you're walking here all by yourself at this young age. Tell me more, where do you come from?

Catherine: It feels like I landed there. It feels like I just walked out of thin air into this place. I'm joyful.

P: What is the most significant observation either within you or around you about this moment?

Catherine: Liberated, free. I see a pond. Water glistening. When I push back the trees the water is there.

P: What do you do next?

Catherine: Breathing, smelling. Smell the earth. Walk.

P: Let the story unfold.

Catherine: My arms are out and I am floating. Standing up, floating above the ground. I went to circle the pond, so beautiful. Just float around the edge. See the light reflecting. I like that.

P: Let us move forward in time to another significant time. What is happening now?

Catherine: I'm in a village, walking in the street.

P: Describe the village to me.

Catherine: The streets are made from stones. There are big stone buildings. The sun is shining on them and on the road. It's flat. It feels like there are people.

P: What do these people look like in terms of dress and culture?

Catherine: Long dresses.

P: What era comes to mind?

Catherine: Like, old. Seventeen-hundreds.

P: What country comes to mind?

Catherine: Scotland.

P: How old are you now?

Catherine: 23.

P: Describe yourself now and what you are doing.

Catherine: I have a dress of short sleeves. A long ribbon around my waist. I'm shorter. I'm walking with my arms to the side, with my palms facing forwards. Walking in the light. Happy. So happy.

P: What makes you such a happy person?

Catherine: I feel free!

P: In what way are you feeling free? Is it an internal experience or is it something in your life that makes you free, or both?

Catherine: It feels like no matter what, nothing can touch me, or take it away.

P: Tell me more about that state.

Catherine: My core feels solid. My heart feels like it is outside of my chest. It surrounds my whole body in some way.

P: How did you get to become so free?

Catherine: In the woods. Being wild in the woods.

P: So something developed in you, something happened within you in the woods that made you this way?

Catherine: I just never felt afraid.

P: You just came into this life this way?

Catherine: Yes.

P: What are you doing in this town now as you're walking around?

Catherine: I'm moving towards the center of the town. There are a square and a fountain. Bright, light water coming out of it. I feel like I want to drink from it and wash my face in it. And watch it. Watch it flow from the earth.

P: What is your living situation? Where do you live and how do you get by?

Catherine: No house. No family.

P: So how do you survive?

Catherine: Kindness. The kindness of others. They feed me.

P: How do you describe yourself? Are you just a free wandering soul who lives by herself and goes around living off the charity of others? A free spirit?

Catherine: Yes. I see a hand with bread. And I turn and listen. I'm grateful.

Throughout this regression, Catherine is highly emotional and in tears. It gets more intense as the session continues.

P: To the eyes of the world, are you an orphan?

Catherine: No.

P: How would you describe it?

Catherine: Free. I feel their hands touching my hands. I make them smile. They love me.

P: What is most significant around or within you about this moment?

Catherine: I feel like I am the fountain. The fountain is me. I feel like I can feel the water in my body and flowing out my body. I feel as I can step into it and be it. And never come out again, and be the fountain.

P: Let us move forward again to a later time in your life, to another significant moment in your life. What is happening now?

Catherine: I'm on a dirt road. There are small fences on either side of it. I'm walking in the green hills on either side. Like the road curves up and I can't see where it goes.

P: How old are you now on this day?

Catherine: 46.

P: Where are you going?

Catherine: See the sheep. Where they live and how they live. They seem to be free but not free.

P: How do they make you feel?

Catherine: It makes me wonder who is caring for them. It makes me feel happy and concerned at the same time.

P: How would you describe yourself, the way you live, what you are?

Catherine: I live with the animals and with nature and we just get along.

P: Do you stay in one place or do you move around a lot?

Catherine: I wander all the time. Walking.

P: What is your state of consciousness throughout this life?

Catherine: I feel a glowing. I feel like my body is the earth. I feel like I sometimes see all of it at once. It's a lot sometimes.

P: Could we say that you are pretty much awakened?

Catherine: Yes.

P: And you came into this birth this way from the beginning?

Catherine: Yes, like I walked out of the sky.

P: What is your purpose in this life?

Catherine: (*even more emotional*) Love. Love. Be love. Walk love.

P: You're 46 years old now, what is the most significant observation about your life at this juncture?

Catherine: I just feel so strong. And fear free. I just know my way, internally and externally. It's all one.

P: In this era, do people, the society around you, just allow you to be who you are, undisturbed? How does the society around you react to your awakening and your free spirit of love?

Catherine: They just know that's who I am. They just say: "O, there she goes." There's just acceptance.

P: Is there anything you do for them or mean to them? And if so, do they understand what you do for them?

Catherine: It's more subtle.

P: Help me understand what that means.

Catherine: By being myself, they are me and I am them. They know that. It's a deep knowing, compassion. Empathy. The empathy is coming up through my feet (*crying out with strong feelings*). Now my heart. I just love them.

P: Let us move forward again to a much later time in your life. What is happening now?

Catherine: I'm sitting on an old stone chair, outside. Very old. There are some trees. I don't see anything else around.

P: How old are you now?

Catherine: 80.

P: What is going on within you now?

Catherine: I'm outside myself, above myself. I see and look down. I'm floating near the sky and I see my body sitting in the chair.

P: Is this a particular state of consciousness?

Catherine: I go in and out of my body and am looking down at the world and the area. There's a grassy meadow around the chair that I didn't see before. There are trees around forming a large circle. They spread out over long distances. This is a secret spot. I see the animals coming. It feels peaceful.

P: Is this something you do more often, stepping out of your body like this?

Catherine: I used to have it happen when I was a teenager and maybe a few times since.

P: What do you do when you step out of your body?

Catherine: It gives me a bigger perspective. I see the world from a different place.

P: When you do this can you also visit other places and meet other people, or do you mostly hover around your body?

Catherine: No, I see the world.

P: The whole world?

Catherine: Yes.

P: So you can basically go wherever you want and see whatever you want to see?

Catherine: Yes.

P: What do you do this for? Is it for learning, understanding or just being?

Catherine: Perspective. It's not about me. It's about the world.

P: How do you feel about yourself now? What's the most significant realization, now being outside the body?

Catherine: We are all free. I am free. We are all together. We have to see each other and all things and all beings. It's like a big concert happening, all at once. But it's not loud. It's like every little tiny thing is happening as it should.

P: You have the realization of this oneness of all existence, yet people are not aware, isn't that true?

Catherine: That is true. There's light coming off my back and my front. It's just emanating out, away from me, towards space. I see her again in the chair. And the light is touching my stomach as I float.

I think she wants me back. I'm going to go back.

P: Back in the body?

Catherine: Yes.

P: What happens next.

Catherine: I feel like I'm sitting a quarter of an inch off the chair. Sitting on a layer of light. There is an energy between my body and the rock, keeping me floating above the rock. I see green things growing around my feet, like vines holding me to the earth.

P: The great Spanish saint Theresa of Avilla had similar things happen to her. The other nuns had to keep her down during prayer so she wouldn't levitate towards the ceiling. Is this something similar?

Catherine: Yes.

P: Let us move to the last day of your life. How old are you now on this last day of your life?

Catherine: Very, very old.

P: Where are you now?

Catherine: There is a big flat slab of stone. It has a base to it, like the stone is set upon this base. It's very old and shaped like an eye. I'm laying on it and I have long grey hair that is flowing in the wind of the sides. There seem to be beings of some kind. Little lights, all around.

P: Are they here to help you ascend?

Catherine: Yes.

P: How does this unfold, the ascension and the transcendence?

Catherine: I feel like I roll onto my side and throw my knees up, like in a fetal position. In the same white gown I wore in the beginning when I first entered the forest. I close my eyes, the sun is shining and the trees are all around. As I close my eyes I feel like I leave my body in the shape that I first came in. I see my body in that shape as I leave. The beings are all around.

P: Before we move on and you describe to me how it all transpires; looking back over this life, what can you tell me about why you took that birth and what the purpose of that life was?

Catherine: The purpose was to somehow spread love. To be joy, to be soul. To touch that.

P: Was there anything for you to learn or was this for the wellbeing of others?

Catherine: I learned to be in nature. I learned about the kindness of people, the earth and animals. I learned the true meaning of sustenance.

P: How do you feel you did?

Catherine: Well.

P: Tell me what happens next?

Catherine: I feel like my arms are above my head, with my hands together. My toes are pointed down. I'm about to take a stroke, like swimming. As I do, like a breaststroke, all the particles of my body come apart and wrap around the planet like in a big giant hug. And I'm just gone. Like a big thank you (*very emotional, weeping*).

I'm part of all of it. Part of everything I saw when I was out of my body. It's like each cell rolls on its back and I can look outward into space. From every point on the earth.

P: Are you staying in this state or are you ascending into a higher consciousness beyond the earth?

Normally, at this point, I guide a client toward the life-between-lives state, helping them cross over. But in this case, I wanted to see what happens if I let her be, as she was describing such amazing cosmic realizations.

> Catherine: It feels like the cells are supposed to stay and see. Be the eyes of the earth, and look into space. Be tethered somehow. The atmosphere can see space through my cells.
>
> P: What about your individual consciousness? Are you able to detach it from these cells, to enter an ascended consciousness beyond the earth plane?
>
> Catherine: Yes, I'm stepped aside from it all. I'm gently held by a force.
>
> P: Allow yourself to enter your spiritual home as you ascend into a higher consciousness...
>
> Catherine: Yes, it's purple. A place to sit. Like I have been gently put down there.
>
> P: What happens next?
>
> Catherine: I'm in a crystal purple place. It's the hall of peace. Beings are around. More shaped like people this time. I feel supported by them.
>
> P: How does it feel right now?
>
> Catherine: Ah, it's so beautiful, so peaceful. It feels solitary but connected.
>
> P: Is this a good place where we can talk about Catherine's life (*her current life*)? And perhaps place this in perspective with life as this free spirit?

Catherine: Yes.

P: If we look at Catherine's life and compare this with your life as this free spirit, what are your observations?

Catherine: They feel the same, but as if in Catherine's life it hasn't been the same.

P: How come?

Catherine: Obstacles to freedom.

P: What would be the cause of obstacles in Catherine's life?

Catherine: People. Their influence. No liberation; pushed and pulled by people.

P: Is it more the collective subconscious of the time Catherine lives in that doesn't support this kind of freedom or is it more that Catherine took upon herself this set of circumstances for a particular reason?

Catherine: Both. She took upon herself the circumstances to take care of everything and everybody around her.

P: Why and to what end?

Catherine: To feel loved and be safe.

P: How do you explain that in your previous life as a free spirit you are so enlightened, while in Catherine's life this doesn't seem to fully manifest? I understand you said it is people and circumstances, but how do you explain this tremendous difference?

Catherine: She got lost to fear of survival, heroism, and details. There seems to be armor. She never worried about survival in the other life.

P: How does it happen, this transition back into confinement, when such high states of spiritual freedom have been attained? How come it hasn't moved into this life of Catherine?

Catherine: Somebody cut it off.

P: Tell me about that.

Catherine: My parents cut it off.

P: If you look at it from this ascended plane, was this cutting-off a karmic cause, or a conscious decision by your soul?

Catherine: It feels like it was the action I had to take at the moment in the womb. I see myself going back to this time in the womb, where my parents were fighting, and I had to take some protective action to save myself.

This is very interesting, because at the beginning of the session when we did a womb regression (which is part of the normal regression process), she described feeling completely engulfed in light, detached and separate from her mother, who was an anxious personality. She described how she was able to be herself and independent in spite of her mother's state of mind. She apparently first entered the womb in an enlightened state but decided to cover it up a while later.

Catherine: That one moment changed everything.

P: What is the next step forward, so you can integrate

the spirit of the awakened consciousness in your previous life, back into Catherine's life?

Catherine: Instead of hanging on to what my parents did I need to let it go and start climbing trees. Be free. I am not them.

P: How do you suggest Catherine does that?

Catherine: I see her sitting there on the tree and everything is falling away. She becomes a ball of light. Her chest is light, drawing something in.

P: Instead of seeing it, can you step into it?

Here Catherine is integrating the experience amidst heavy sighs of relief. I leave her be for a while. She is going through a very deep and emotional experience.

Catherine: All light. Everything has fallen away. I'm back into the purple crystal space. A light is coming from there onto my life as Catherine. It is shining on the whole life.

A light is shining in the line of that life. There are lots of colors that are brighter than the earth itself. All those years are bright and colorful now. Along the timeline (*heavy emotional breathing*).

P: Is the integration complete now?

Catherine: Yes.

P: How do you feel now?

Catherine: Wonderful. I feel great.

P: Could we say that the awakening of the previous

life has been re-integrated back into Catherine's awareness now?

Catherine: Yes I feel liberated. I'm standing up with my arms stretched out and my palms up. Like I used to. I feel really tall. I feel like I just want to keep walking that way. Walking into space. No need to go anywhere. Just walk. My chest out, shoulders back.

I'm flying now. Feeling the air. I feel the energy going across my body. It's so easy to move here. Every motion turns into light. I turn into light. I feel like a star falling. Falling through space (*ecstatic*). I am one with all the other light.

Sooo peaceful.

P: Is there more to be explored or are you ready?

Catherine: I'm ready. I feel clean.

I gently let her re-integrate back into her body and we slowly end the session. Catherine let me know after the session how her life has profoundly changed and how she has her inner awakening and freedom back. She told me that most probably the rest of her life is needed to fully integrate what happened during the session.

Considering the fact that she attained a highly advanced state of consciousness in a previous body, and that her current body and her current environment are not used to this high vibration, it is understandable that full integration may take time.

What is very interesting about this case is that it seems she lost her high state of consciousness in the womb. When she first entered the womb she still carried with her the light of her previous attainment, but in order to adapt to her new environment and shield herself, she chose to cover it.

A great saint once told me that spiritual enlightenment is not just an individual affair. The collective subconscious of our culture and our body must be attuned enough to carry its high frequency. In our western world, it has been very hard, if not impossible, to attain such superconscious states. Only a select few were powerful enough. The collective simply didn't support such states. But things seem to be changing now, and everywhere, like mushrooms in a forest, these enlightened beings are popping up, piercing the previously impenetrable density of our modern time.

This applies to our body and nervous system too. The food we eat, the people we hang out with, the vibratory field of our parents and caregivers, all these influences the environment of emerging consciousness. Catherine is learning how to carry this current through her body and express it freely in her environment. We are not separate from our environment. An enlightened being, especially, is highly sensitive not only within but also to the world around. We are all connected.

Energetically this makes sense too. We are, after all, not matter. Quantum physics teaches us that only energy exists. As Albert Einstein said:

"We are slowed down sound and light waves, a walking bundle of frequencies tuned into the cosmos. We are souls dressed up in a sacred biochemical garment and our bodies are the instruments through which our souls play their music."

Irrespective of all of the above, and no matter what impression this and the following case may leave on the reader, what matters most is the transformative results that occur during this experience for the client. In both these cases, the transformation was enormous and lasting. As a matter of fact, during these sessions, the energy was so powerful that it had a permanent effect on me, the therapist, as well.

The following case is that of a 34-year-old woman called June, from Northern California, who came to see me in my Southern California office. Though born and raised in the United States and from American parents, her delicate features seemed Middle Eastern. With a very open and cheerful personality, she carried an internal light with her the moment she walked through the door.

Even in this life she had done a lot of spiritual practices, was teaching, and was actively involved in the yoga world. A mother of two young kids, she had found what she called her 'twin-soul' and was very happy and steady in her family and love life.

Yet she was searching for more. On her intake form, she expressed her need to connect to a higher power and felt a strong inner call to manifest a higher consciousness. What happened next was much more than she could have ever imagined.

During her regression, we first went back to the womb, where we had some interesting events. Her first thoughts in the womb were: "Not again! What am I doing here again!"

June: I'm feeling constricted. It's nice and warm but I know what is about to happen.

P: What is your assessment of the body you're going to be working with?

June: It'll do. It's sufficient and healthy.

P: What are the best qualities of this body?

June: My skin feels nice. The body is going to be healthy and strong. To protect how sensitive I'm going to be.

P: What about the brain you're going to be using this time around?

June: It's going to be misunderstood often. It's not of this world.

P: Tell me more?

June: It's like a high-speed processor. There are not many words to use to describe it. It retains and accesses information at a higher rate. People are going to find it really odd, all the things you can remember.

P: How do you feel with it?

June: It's pure. It streams divine consciousness, like a portal, a channel of truth. That's what I'm afraid of.

P: Why would you be afraid of that?

June: Because people don't like the truth.

P: On the one hand there are people and on the other hand there is you and the people that you love. What about you and how it works for you?

June: If you take everybody else out of the equation it is simple. It gives me all the answers to everything in the universe.

I don't like being separated. Every time I'm born I'm being separated. From the source, this peace.

P: Could this mind and body be used to channel the source, so you're not so separated?

June: Yes, but I'm still alone.

P: Why alone?

June: I feel alone around others. In this state, I'm full and unified. Everyone else mirrors the separation. It's hard. Here I feel connected.

June was already plugged into a higher consciousness from the womb and we progressed straight into the life-between-lives dimension. This is not uncommon, and even from here we can still access past-life information when required. For some souls, the past-life experience is not so relevant at this stage in their evolution and the soul chooses to ascend right away. The fact that we scheduled this session on this particular day has relevance too. It is at this moment in time that an experience is required to gain insight into how to continue the journey of this life. A pitstop or, a checkpoint, where the soul checks back in and connects to the source to get an updated map or receive more fuel to continue the journey.

June: The frequency I feel running through my body right now is not human. It is much higher.

P: Embrace the non-physicality of your being.

June: Aaah, this is a very weird feeling. There is not much gravity (*breathing heavily, and starting to weep*). This is what I missed (*sobbing, entering an ecstatic cosmic state instantly*). It's so much better here (*crying loudly*).

I didn't think it was going to be so hard down there (*still sobbing*). I don't want to go anymore. I'm sort of here but not here.

P: Yes, these are parallel existences, parallel frequencies. These co-exist. It's not a location. It's a frequency, a state of consciousness.

What are you noticing within and around you right now?

June: It's just less dense. My body doesn't necessarily stay in form. I can shape-shift. I can be here in a form if I want it to be. There is no need to survive.

P: Is there any presence or energy near you that we may regard as a guiding principle? Or are you your own guiding principle?

June: Yes, my own. There is a lot of freedom. I keep

seeing a lot of blue, turquoise and purple colors.

P: Are these your own energies or those of energies around you?

June: These are the colors of other beings.

P: Is this a good place to ask some questions about June's life, since you are so connected to your highest consciousness?

June: (*Laughing*) She's fine.

P: Well, shall we just ask it because that's what she came here to do today?

June: Ok, why not.

P: June is asking whether she should teach some spiritual and relational concepts she has been thinking about.

June: Just being born is really all you need to do. You hold seeds of consciousness. That impact, the presence, and what you choose to do with it with your free will is enough. She is trying to find a sense of purpose but that is not the point.

P: Just being?

June: Yes.

P: Is she aware of this in her day-to-day awareness?

June: Sometimes, but June has a lot of drive and determination, trying to find an earthly purpose.

P: How do you suggest she can find a middle path? (*A long silence as she goes deeper within*).

June: I feel I'm going into a different space now. I keep

seeing the image of Jesus. Not the real image, only the image that we have been shown.

I don't understand why. I feel nauseated (*emotional*). Upset.

P: How come?

June: It's a lie. They used me. This isn't how it was supposed to be.

P: How come you are able to feel this pain? What is your relationship with that?

June: (*weeping*) I don't want to say.

P: Just say it, there is nobody here.

June: (*weeping louder*) Nobody will believe me. It was me (weeping hard and long, shaking). My whole body is on fire, (*continuing to weep loudly and for a long time*).

I don't know what is happening.

P: Just accept it.

June: I don't want to (*weeping loudly still*).

P: Just let it be, don't resist. You're a channel. That's right. Moving with you and moving through you.

She has a hard time taking in the current of the divine energy that suddenly has started to move through her. It takes a while and with some help and encouragement she is finally able to calm down and let it flow through more easily.

June: (*still ecstatic*) They're showing me that love is all there is. I don't need to do anything. I'll be moved when I'm moved from the heart (*shaking and breathing heavy for the next few more minutes*).

I never wanted to be idolized. I'm afraid I'm going to mess it all up again. There is something I don't know.

Oh man. It's a sacrifice, to come back and to see where we are. I can't be present often. It feels a little traumatic. From the in-between state, where it is so beautiful. I'm having a hard time finding that beauty here. But I want to. Every time I come in, the world isn't very kind to me. Because of what I represent. I get burned or I get hung. So I hide. I isolate. I dumb myself down, but then I don't love myself when I do that.

I'm learning that's more important. To love my self first.

This can't be true (*a part of her own self intermingles with the force that is moving through her. I stepped in to help her*).

P: Of course it can be. Spirit can move through you. It's not a body. It's a consciousness that connects with you. This is how mediums work. He is not one person. He could be working through millions like you. You're tapping into his reality right now. This is what happens with saints. They channel. Do you know about the people that had the stigmata? That's you now. Just take it, don't doubt yourself.

June: (*weeping louder*) They keep trying to tell me that. I'm so afraid.

P: Take it. Let it go. You can take it quietly and silently. Nobody needs to know. In the background. Let him work through you in the background. He is so big. He doesn't work in just one body. Whoever is ready to take his love.....

June: I keep hearing there is an actual number. Around 200.000 people. This isn't the first time this has happened.

P: Take a moment to allow this force to normalize your nervous system.

June: What's interesting is the other beings around me were even higher. I couldn't be with them for very long. This one I can actually integrate.

P: Maybe their energy is too high for our nervous system? Like 10.000 Volts running through a little wire?

June: Yes that's what they said. I got a little of it though. It's still communicating to me, but differently, more through the mind. But what it is saying is that the goal is for me to actually embody them in this lifetime. Fully bringing them into my human being. But that it is going to take time. But that's the purpose. When you asked me this question earlier; that's the purpose. They want to enter into me fully.

P: I understand.

June: I can't now. My body is not ready.

P: Yes, you may need to do practices to get ready.

June: Yes that's what they say. They're saying that the Jesus frequency is actually a match right now. I can actually integrate this one and be ok and not get sick. But the next step is coming. I already quit drinking and stop eating meat. The reason I'm cutting my relationships with most people right now isn't isolation but a requirement. They want me to move away to a more suitable place with better vibrations, less interference in the energetic waves.

They say that at that point I should start growing my own food and start to become one with the purity of the earth. At that time they will allow themselves to enter into me more deeply.

Now I have a sense of purpose. That's what I've been looking for (*she is slowly coming down from the ecstatic state and re-integrating with her physical self*).

I let her be with the divine energy for a bit and allow things to settle and integrate more deeply and ask her to let me know when she is ready. As she is enjoying the peace and bliss she suddenly says:

June: Oh my God, they are all here. Saint Germaine, a whole bunch of them showing themselves to me in a human form, so I can see, cheering me on. Like: 'you can do it!' Sometimes I don't feel like I can do it.

P: Isn't that the 'I' talking? What about being just a vessel?

June: Yes, They tell me they wouldn't be here if I would be a being that would do that. They are choosing the meek, the humble.

I don't want to say goodbye.

P: I'm not in a hurry. Take your time.

After a while, we finally bring the session to an end.

The notion that a divine figure works through many souls is not a new concept. Only when you look upon a historical figure as a body or an individual does this idea seems unrealistic. But is Jesus just a body or is he made out of spirit, one with the ultimate consciousness from which he emerged? We referred in an earlier chapter to the idea of how ice, gas, mist are all different forms of water, and that similarly, out of the ocean of infinite consciousness, saints emerge that can take up a human body for the sake of humanity.

June, through her innate innocence and purity of character, was able to connect to the frequency of divine beings, who choose her to start to work with and through her. I've personally heard of this concept many times while I lived in India so the event, as it occurred during the session, wasn't novel or strange to me, and accordingly I was able to help her make sense of what was happening to her.

If you think of it, it would make perfect sense that a divine source would want to work through more souls at once. In order to raise the frequency of our world, why work through only one powerful avatar, when you can work through hundreds of thousands of other vessels at once?

We can all be such vessels. Illumination is a gradual process, like the opening of a lotus flower. To the extent the bud opens, we become channels of divine consciousness. It is not the birthright of a few privileged souls, it is the true nature of who we are.

Pure souls like Catherine and June are just a bit ahead

of most of us, ushering in a new age of consciousness. Through their help, we too can get closer to living a divine life and start to manifest the divine within our own conscious reality. I consider it a rare and blessed opportunity to meet such souls and to witness closeup their ecstatic states of being. They are beacons of hope and light, encouraging us to look not only upon ourselves as potentially divine beings, but to also look at society at large as an emerging awakening consciousness on earth.

Chapter 16
Re-Connecting Our Divine Purpose

Kim, 32 years old, came to see me in my office in Boone, North Carolina. Born in Korea, she was a very sweet and quiet personality, with questions about her life that revolved around her health and her purpose. She had unexplained health issues that no medical doctor could find a cause for, and she had a hard time opening up and connecting with people. Her parents had been very strict and physical with her and even today she was afraid of displeasing them. She has been trying to conceive a child but has so far been unsuccessful.

This case had several similarities with the case in the previous chapter, where Catherine had, in this life, completely lost the awareness of her previously attained a high state of consciousness, and needed to reawaken the power of her own true Self. And, like Catherine, Kim's past life too had great repercussions in this life.

We pick up this story at the beginning of the past-life regression.

Kim: It's daytime. I'm outside and alone.

P: What is the first thing that you notice?

Kim: Mountains. Snow peaked high mountains. It's spring. My cabin is here.

P: Can you describe this cabin to me?

Kim: It's made of wood. Very small. I live here alone.

P: Can you describe what it looks like inside?

Kim: There are herbs hanging. For medication.

P: Is that for personal use or for others?

Kim: For personal use.

P: Are you familiar with these kinds of medicinal herbs?

Kim: Yes. I'm alone. I need to survive.

P: When you go outside, how do you feel?

Kim: It's cold. I love it here.

P: What's most significant about this moment?

Kim: I can see very big and dark green pine trees. I can

hear a stream. There is nobody around me.

P: How do you feel about that?

Kim: Peaceful.

P: Why are you alone in this forest?

Kim: I chose this life.

P: Why?

Kim: I can be free. I cannot be with negative energies.

P: What is your state of mind like?

Kim: Very peaceful. Very good.

P: Do you feel connected to a higher energy when you are here? (*A bit of a leading question, but I felt that she entered a higher state of consciousness already, so I took the leap*).

Kim: Yes.

P: What is your internal state of mind now?

Kim: I'm a medium (*suddenly becoming very emotional and breathing hard*). I came here to be with nature. I know how to live with animals. They speak to me. The earth.

P: How does this make you feel?

Kim: (*Breathing very heavily and in an ecstatic state*) I'm part of them.

P: Be with it for a moment (*she cries intensely and deeply in ecstatic bliss. I leave her for a moment*).

Kim: I'm a woman.

P: How old are you now?

Kim: 40.

P: Which country are you in?

Kim: Somewhere in Europe, in the mountains of Germany. The sky is pale.

P: At what time?

Kim: 1500

P: Do people come to you or are you living by yourself?

Kim: No, by myself.

P: Moving forward in time till you're older, to another relevant moment in life. What is happening now?

Kim: Oh, eh. I'm sick.

P: How old are you now?

Kim: 50.

P: Where are you now?

Kim: In the cabin. I'm coughing.

P: How serious is it?

Kim: I'm ready to move on.

P: Please move to the last day of your life. Are you still in the cabin?

Kim: (*Coughing loudly. This is unusual. Though clients often get completely immersed in the session [they can also be a witness from above or afar], they rarely display the physical symptoms of their last life in their current body. For example, they rarely, if ever, speak their mother tongue [of the last life] during the session. They do display all the emotions and sometimes voice intonations*).

P: Ok let the coughing go. Let it pass (*coughing passes immediately*). What is going on right now?

Kim: I'm on the bed.

P: How are you feeling?

Kim: I'm weak.

P: Tell me about your life and how you lived it.

Kim: I am so scared of people. They will kill me, as a witch. I needed to run away. I was not part of them. I was scared. I was not like them. I am peaceful.

I want to go back home (*the afterlife*).

P: After you ran away from home, how was your life in the forest?

Kim: I needed to hide. I couldn't show myself to people.

P: How did this make you feel?

Kim: I was happy. People don't understand. They don't know how I was different. They don't know. They don't know. I'm connected to everyone and everything around me. To every animal. To nature.

P: How was your internal state, spiritually.

Kim: So at peace. So confident. I know who I am. I know. I know what I'm doing. I know.

P: Was it a good life?

Kim: Yes!!

P: What did you like best about it?

Kim: I survived. I survived. I wasn't burned. I survived,

I ran away.

P: At what age did you run away?

Kim: Ah, very young. 16.

P: What powers did you have at that age that made you ran away?

Kim: I saw women burned.

P: And you were afraid that would happen to you?

Kim: Yes.

P: Were people around you already aware of who you were at that time in your life?

Kim: Yes. My family and friends knew who I was. I couldn't trust them. They would burn me. I had to run away.

P: What was it that you were doing, so young?

Kim: I can see the future. I know what happens. I couldn't tell anybody. They'd betray me.

P: What did you learn most during this life?

Kim: I feel safe with nature. I can't trust people. They are not ready yet.

I move her to the moment just after she died.

P: Where are you now, in relation to the body you just left behind?

Kim: I'm floating above it. I can see the cabin.

P: How are you feeling now?

Kim: I'm feeling great! I'm at peace.

P: How do you feel about your death?

Kim: I was not scared, I was happy.

P: What was your last thought when you left the body?

Kim: I was alone in life, but I was happy.

P: Before we move on, is there any unattended business you need to attend to, anybody you need to see or are you ready to move on now?

Kim: I want to go.

I help her move to the in-between-life state.

Kim: I'm alone. I'm walking through the door of a building that looks like a dome.

P: What happens next?

Kim: I need to go inside.

P: What is inside?

Kim: People, waiting for me.

P: What or who are these people?

Kim: The Council.

P: How many Council members are here?

Kim: Many.

P: Can you count them?

Kim: 12.

P: Is there anybody stepping forward from amongst the Council members?

Kim: Yes, a woman. She's my guardian.

P: Is she one of the Council members?

Kim: No. She's my guardian.

She welcomes me. The Council members are sitting at the table. A round table in a semi-circle.

The guardian is smiling. She's an African woman, with curly hair. I love her eyes.

P: Do you know her?

Kim: I think so.

P: What happens next?

Kim: A Council member asks me how my life was.

P: Which of the Council members is asking you this?

Kim: The one in the middle.

P: Is it a male, female or an androgynous kind of energy?

Kim: Male.

P: What does he look like?

Kim: An old man. He asks how my life was.

P: What do you say?

Kim: It was ok.

P: What does the Council member say about it?

Kim: You did a great job.

P: What did they like about it?

Kim: That I didn't give up.

P: Is there any constructive criticism offered, about

things that you may perhaps have done differently?

Kim: They say that I should have more courage.

(*Council speaking now. Sometimes the client, when in this state, hears the Council or a guide speak and relays it to me, and at other times it takes over and talks directly*) You shouldn't hide all your life. You are gifted. We gave you power. We were with you. You should help people.

P: What is your reaction?

Kim: I was scared. I was weak. I was all alone. I was with no one.

(*Council speaking*) We are with you. You need to stand up. You are gifted.

P: What else do they offer in terms of advice, or observation?

Kim: (*Council speaking*) You need to learn how to love people. You need to learn how to live with people. You're not alone. You need to stand up. Your gift is for helping people, not hiding. You know how to communicate with us. You need to step up. You need to challenge your fears and obstacles.

P: But what about the society you lived in? What could you have done?

Kim: I told them. I told them that they are very ignorant. That they are not ready. Human beings are not ready. They need more time for evolution.

P: What do they say to that?

Kim: (*Council speaking*) That's why we sent you there,

to speed things up. Religions are not the answer (*particular relevant during the burning of witches in the middle ages*). You need to forget their ignorance. Your mission is helping them, not hiding. Forget about yourself.

Kim again: I was scared.

Sorry.

P: Was that the plan that you had set out to achieve before taking this birth?

Kim: Yes, they said I was qualified.

But I was not ready.

P: So the plan was not really fulfilled?

Kim: No. They are disappointed. They are nice, they are like my parents, but they want me to do more. They want me to speed things up.

P: Ok, why you? What makes you special?

Kim: I'm not special.

P: What makes you qualified?

Kim: I had experience. A lot.

P: Where did this experience come from?

Kim: From my past.

P: Past lives?

Kim: Yes.

P: What can you tell me about this past?

Kim: I didn't live like a normal human. I was always with God.

P: Did these qualities develop in the in-between state or on earth?

Kim: On earth.

P: You were always with God?

Kim: Yes, there (*on earth*) and also when I was in-between lives.

P: What is your specialty as a soul?

Kim: Healing and medicine. I can show them how to evolve.

P: So you're a teacher?

Kim: Yes.

P: Do you belong to a particular soul group?

Kim: I don't have a soul group. I work with the guardian and the Council directly.

P: What was the plan for Kim's life, before taking this birth?

Kim: She needs to learn and understand people. She was always with God and in nature. That is not helpful for her.

P: So this life revolves around that?

Kim: Yes, learning to understand. That's why she is with a family who cannot understand her. This way she learns about people and their issues.

P: Did Kim bring some of these healing qualities with her this time?

Kim: (*emphatically*) Yea!

P: Is she using these already?

Kim: No.

P: Why not?

Kim: She's locked up.

P: How can she unlock these again? Is she supposed to?

Kim: Yes!!!

P: If we ask the Council now about Kim's life plan, what do they say?

Kim: She needs to open her gifts, her chakras.

P: How can she do that?

Kim: She needs to remember her past lives, who she is.

P: Can we do this right here, and can the Council help us with this?

Kim: They give me a light. But they say that we can show you the light, but that you need to do this yourself. Because this is your mission.

P: Can you describe the mission again?

Kim: Open the chakras. Open the gifts. And heal yourself first. Then you can heal others.

P: Are you going to do that?

Kim: Yes.

P: Why did you choose a Korean body and a female body this time (*one of Kim's pre-session questions*)?

Kim: Korean society is harsh on women. She always chooses the body of a woman because it is easier to communicate with God. The Korean women's body was the best challenge. The Korean woman suffers a lot of obstacles.

P: So this challenge, being a Korean woman, helps you open up the chakras?

Kim: Yes. An easy path doesn't help her.

P: Is that why you also choose this family and its problems?

Kim: Definitely.

P: This was planned?

Kim: Yes, They are different souls, a different group. But she chose them deliberately for this purpose.

P: Why does Kim feel so alone in this birth (*another one of her pre-session questions*)?

Kim: Because of her memories. She belongs to a different realm.

P: How come she suffers from these physical problems, while nobody can diagnose the causes of this?

Kim: It's an imbalance. An imbalance between mind and body.

P: What caused this?

Kim: Negative thinking.

P: Where did this begin? Because when we look at your life as this enlightened healer, connected to God, when even in the in-between-life you belong to God, we don't seem to see any negativity.

Kim: Her gift is for helping people. But she is afraid of people. So her gifts get locked up because of this fear.

P: So this is what's causing these issues?

Kim: Yes.

P: So it's not a physical cause but a spiritual one?

Kim: Yes!!

P: What does she need to do now to unlock this?

Kim: She needs to get rid of this fear.

P: How can we achieve that?

Kim: She needs to be part of people. She belongs to them too.

P: What about her husband and her relationship with him (*whom in her intake form she wrote about lovingly*)?

Kim: He heals her. He understands her. She was always alone. But this time she needs to learn to be together with someone. So this was planned.

P: What about her struggle to conceive a child? What can the Council tell us about this?

Kim: They say that if you want to learn more you can have children, but it's not essential. For now, you need to look at other people as your children. They are also your children.

P: Are there any karmas standing in her way (*this is one of her pre-session questions*)?

Kim: (*Ignoring the question, the Council speaks*) We are all connected. We are all family. Don't think about your own children. You think about your mission, why you came to this earth. We count on you.

P: What again is this mission for this life?

Kim: Educating people. They need to wake up spiritually. They need to change. Stop all the negativity.

P: What is the specialty of your gift? Is it healing or foresight?

Kim: Healing. Foresight is not meaningful for now.

P: Physical healing?

Kim: Physical and mental healing.

P: Does food play a roll in this (*another one of her pre-session questions*)?

Kim: Yes she needs to eat more vegetables. That's what she has been doing in her past lives. Don't count on modern medicines, these are toxic. She knows what to do. She still has the knowledge; she knows.

P: Can she still communicate with nature like before?

Kim: She is locked up this time.

P: Can she unlock it again this time?

Kim: If she can let go of fear.

(*Council speaking*) She is so pure. She needs to protect herself. We are always here. But we cannot protect her all the time. She needs to cooperate too. Avoid toxic, negative and violent media.

She needs to be independent. She needs to stand up and build up her defenses.

P: So if we summarize this correctly, she needs, on the one hand, to open her heart to connect with people and love them, while on the other hand build her defenses against negativity like toxic foods and media?

Kim: Always balance, always balance.

P: She seems to have a lot of dreams about ancestors. What can you share about that (*another pre-session question*)?

Kim: That's because she is a medium. She can still communicate with them even today.

P: Can she still work as a medium in this life?

Kim: That's not her mission in this life. She can use it to learn about people, to know who they are. In dreams, she can be free.

P: Now that we are still with the Council, can we ask them what we may have missed today and what may be of importance to Kim's life (*A very important question as it allows for insights that the client, even in a superconscious state, is unaware of*)?

Kim: (*Council speaking*) You're still hiding. You are running away from people again. Because you know what they are thinking; you know what they are going to do; you see so many things. Do - not - run - away !! Don't run away this time. That's why we gave you a good life. It's much easier than your previous lives. You have a partner. You are safe now. And you want to run away again!!! Not this time!! If you want to learn more you shouldn't run away.

P: There is no excuse to be afraid this time is there?

Kim: No.

P: How do you feel about what you are hearing?

Kim: I can feel their great love. I understand why.

P: Do you feel equipped and ready to take on that challenge now?

Kim: Yes.

P: Is there anything you need from the Council to accomplish this mission?

Kim: They count on me. I will take on more responsibilities after this life.

P: What kind of responsibilities?

Kim: I will guide more souls. I will teach them, lead them.

P: On earth or in-between lives?

Kim: In-between lives.

P: So this life is dedicated to free and open yourself?

Kim: Last chance, it's the last chance.

P: Are you ready for that?

Kim: Yes.

P: Is there anything you would like from the Council that we haven't discussed yet?

Kim: What should I do from now onwards?

(*Council speaking*) Do anything you want, but work with people. You can do anything because you have many experiences. You are so good at helping.

P: So it doesn't matter what work you do as long as you work with people and stick to the mission, opening your heart?

Kim: Yes.

P: Anything else we may have missed?

Kim: They are not the talkative types.

P: The spirit world is wide open to you. Is there anywhere else you'd like to go?

Kim: I just like to go around.

P: Ok go ahead and tell me where you are going first.

Kim: I'd like a few moments alone with them (*the Council*).

P: Ok please go and do that and let me know when you are ready (*very long silence – she is breathing heavily during this time*).

Kim: I'm recharging.

P: Is this with the Council?

Kim: Yes, they are giving me power. I did it myself.

P: The recharge? How did you do this?

Kim: They surrounded me. They showed me a light. The light comes through my head through to my feet. I did it myself.

P: How do you feel now?

Kim: Great. Opened up.

P: What happens now?

Kim: I'm ready to get back.....

We slowly end the session here.

She wrote to me after the session: " Thank you for helping me remember who I am." Kim's extraordinary journey through time and space is a beautiful example of how a soul comes into this life with a higher purpose, and how this purpose can take many lifetimes to accomplish. Like Catherine, Kim had forgotten this purpose and the true nature of her being. Her physical and mental struggles were caused by this forgetfulness as well as being out of alinement with her true purpose.

It is hard to describe on paper the beauty and depth of these souls, as they open up to their true Selves. Kim, to all outside appearances, looks like a shy and timid Korean woman, but on the inside, she is an ancient and accomplished healer. Her divine journey, having always lived with God and with nature, is an attempt to connect to her fellow human beings in order to help them on their evolutionary path.

She seems sent by the Council of higher beings to help us on our way, yet even this experiment takes several lives to accomplish, with an unsuccessful life in between. This life as Kim seems to be a transitional life, with the particular aim to teach her how to learn to relate to ordinary people and their problems. Being with God, and a child of nature, it is understandable how her pure soul finds it hard to adjust to the sometimes violent nature of our world. She has been given a hard task.

It reminds me of June's case when she channeled the Christ energy, who had an equally hard time accepting the tremendous sacrifice to his higher nature while being sent to earth to help others.

Most of us just try to become more enlightened, but Kim

already had attained a high degree of divine consciousness in earlier lives. For her, the challenge was to learn to integrate it into our denser earth environment, with the intent of helping others. The Council of higher beings clearly cared greatly about this mission and challenged Kim not to give up and to get her act together. June, in the previous chapter, had a similar task.

Things and people are mostly not what and whom they seem to be. Behind each soul is an infinite journey. And behind all our problems lies a greater master plan.

Kim, by reconnecting to the Council of great beings, was being reminded that her problems on earth were caused by something much different than she thought.

It is a beautiful reminder for all of us, that often the cause of our problems is that we are out of touch with our larger divine purpose. We are trying to solve the symptoms of particular issues, without truly understanding the true reasons why things happen in our lives. That, more often than not, first and foremost, the problems are a reminder to turn within and discover why we are on earth and what we need to do.

Trying to fix problems without understanding our greater cause is not going to be effective. Kim was having health problems and tried every medical method available, but was unsuccessful even diagnosing the causes of what ails her. During the session, she learned that her health problems were merely a symptom of her spiritual disconnect with her true Self and her higher spiritual goals.

It cannot be overstated how important it is to be in sync with our highest purpose. Because once you are, you can subordinate the smaller issues to the larger cause. You have a frame of reference. It is hard to make any meaningful life's decisions if you don't know what your true purpose is. Smaller goals, like being secure, finding our life's partner, having meaningful work, tend to become our main focus. We dedicate a disproportionate amount of time and resources to minor goals, thereby eventually becoming disoriented and out of balance. Once this unbalance occurs we try to fix the issues related to the smaller goals, without being aware that the real cause was a lack of awareness of our soul's true purpose. Had you focussed more on establishing inner balance by aligning your goals to your soul's purpose, you wouldn't have had many of the issues you are trying to solve in the first place. And even if you have issues, you would have a healthy perspective, and be able to subordinate these issues to things that are more important.

By reconnecting to her true identity and purpose, Kim is able to understand who she is and what she needs to do. She now knows that her family is there to help her connect to others and teach her sympathy. She also understands now that her health problems are caused by an imbalance and that once she re-establishes inner balance her health will get better. By remembering her past life, she has gained more insight into why her tendency is to shy away from people, and that rather than giving in to this tendency, it is critically important for her to reach out and open her heart. She even was given a glimpse of the life that will follow Kim's life and her overall divine purpose as a healer and guide of souls.

It is very hard to know your purpose if you never have felt the divinity of your own soul. If all that you know about yourself is what you seem to be looking at in the mirror, you are looking from the outside in, rather than from the inside out. By going beyond all the external conditions of their apparent personality, the three women in this and in the last chapter became re-awakened to who they really are. They felt once again that the personality they seem to be, and the role they play here on earth, is but one of many masks they wear, but that beyond these masks they are instruments of the divine source energy.

If even for a moment, you are able to see beyond the world we live in to connect to something transcendental, your life can change instantly. Because you have, through your own personal experience, learned to understand that there is something else, something higher. This realization alone can be transformative and set you free from your day to day struggles that have totally occupied your mind space. If I know that my true identity is immortal and that my true home is transcendental, I will know that there is a way out of my problems and apparent limitations. And that I have the potential to be really free, once and for all. At this point it is not just a belief, faith or even hope anymore, it is an actual inner knowing.

Conclusion

Chapter 17

Climbing The Mountain

Many of the extraordinary cases described in this book are from clients who have done a lot of internal work before they came to see me. It is a misunderstanding to think that these people are special or privileged. They came better prepared with calm nervous systems and minds, which helps us access the inner recesses of their being more easily. Also, they have worked on clearing out subconscious blocks and debris.

These blocks manifest at three levels; the body, the mind

(and subconscious) and the karmic waves that keep crashing the shores of our conscious mind. I like to address each of these three aspects, beginning with the body. The removal of these blocks not only helps you establish a better connection with your higher nature but also helps in preparation for your life-between-lives session.

Most of us are busy and directing much of our energy and attention outward, trying to navigate through what is happening in our lives. If I were to put sensors on you to measure your brain's activity during this busy time, I'd most probably find your mind in a Beta state. The Beta state is what we call cognitive awareness. It's like driving at night on a narrow country road in the pitch dark. It's so dark that you cannot even see yourself sitting in the car. Your full and undivided attention is required to stay on the road. Your internal awareness is completely subordinate to your external awareness. You're so focused on the road and staying alive that you are hardly aware of yourself.

In order to calm your mind down, and turn the headlights from the road towards your internal awareness, certain things are required. What one experiences during a life-between-life session is a re-direction of attention from the outside to the inside. We aim for you to be hyper-aware of your own internal Self and greatly reduce, yet not de-activate, your external awareness.

We do not completely disconnect your external awareness because this guardian aspect of your mind is required to keep you safe at all times. If an alarm sounds or you have to go to the bathroom, this aspect of your mind warns you.

This guardian is what keeps things noble. This means that at no time during the session would you lose a sense of ownership of your own state of being.

This is an aspect of hypnotic regression that is often misunderstood. What we are trying to achieve is hyper-awareness, the complete opposite of losing awareness, unlike during surgery when you are administered an anesthetic and become unconscious. During a regression session you gain tremendous inner awareness, but not at the expense of outside awareness. The outside is simply relaxed to the background. If required, it is able to present itself at a moments notice to intervene.

This switch from external focus towards internal awareness is a process that works differently for each and every person. I'm a firm believer that everyone is capable of this. We are a soul with our body and mind wrapped around it. So to assume that you are not able to get in touch with your own Self would imply that some people have a soul and others do not. While this may seem hard to see in some, the soul exists but is sometimes deeply buried and so not as apparent.

If someone struggles to turn within during a past life regression while others don't, the reason is that not everyone is equally prepared. This chapter helps you understand and become aware of what it takes to open yourself up to this inner awareness.

When my wife Jenna, a Yoga and Massage therapist and a gifted energy healer, and I conduct a past-life regression workshop, we slowly guide the group through certain carefully planned exercises. These exercises and practices are designed to help the group get prepared for what is to come: the past-life regression.

In order to get the maximum benefit from an LBL session, a similar preparation is required. Though I have had many great LBL sessions with people who had little or no preparation, I have noticed over the years there are better results with those who come prepared.

The body is a beautiful instrument that houses our mind and nervous system. Our higher Self is beyond this body. Yet in order to access this higher Self, we need to work through our body and with our mind. It stands to reason therefore that this body and the mind need to be suitable conduits.

Collectively we're aware of the meaning of physical health and wellbeing. But when it comes to preparing the body as a conduit for divine consciousness more than just good health is required. Our nervous system needs to be calmed down. What we eat and drink has a great effect on our nervous system. Eating hot and spicy food stimulates the nervous system and makes it restless. Eating heavy, fatty foods makes the nervous system more dense and lethargic. We generally think of food in term of physical health, but we seem less aware of the innate properties of food in regards to the effect it has on our nervous system and mind. When we try to access a higher frequency, these subtle properties of food become an integral part of our preparation.

Conclusion

If you were to eat super spicy chicken wings the evening before a session, it is more likely that the next morning you are going to be restless as your stomach and nervous system are more excited than you want them to be. This also applies to stimulants like coffee or caffeine.

A sensitive nervous system is imperative if you want to develop a finely attuned communion with higher consciousness. It's like the refinement of crude oil. Unrefined crude oil is good for greasing engines. When you refine it you get petrol for your car. When you refine it more you get fuel suitable for race cars. An even greater refinement creates rocket fuel. Your nervous system can carry higher and more powerful currents of consciousness when it is sufficiently refined.

At a certain moment in our spiritual life, we become more aware of the need to create a different kind of lifestyle. As this refinement takes place you become more aware of the reactions certain foods and drinks have on your overall state of mind. At first, this awareness may just be physical, but as you develop, you become so finely tuned that you react mentally to what you ingest. It's a double-edged sword. On the one hand, you become more finely attuned, on the other hand, you also become much more sensitive.

It is difficult to be more specific as to what is a suitable and what is an unsuitable diet because this is highly personal. It is something to experiment with along the way as we learn to listen to our own body and mind and make the required adjustments. What works best for you is the best diet. What matters is that we learn to ask ourselves, does this help me feel and function better? The priorities of an Olympic athlete will be different than those of a yogi who craves for cosmic consciousness so diets are adjusted accordingly.

The second important aspect that needs our attention is the mind. Food and diet affect the mind. But what we 'consume' in terms of media intake affects us too. Living in our modern world is very different than living two hundred years ago. We get bombarded day and night by an ever-increasing onslaught of external impulses. It would be naive to think that this has no effect on our mind and nervous system. It affects us on two levels. On the one hand, and more directly, it stimulates our minds and keeps it in perpetual motion. The waves of data keep overwhelming the calm interior harbor of our being.

But at a deeper level, these media impulses start shaping our belief system and our worldview, even determining what we eat, need, crave and plan for. These artificially create certain needs, which are restless waves of desires, that then we start working for in order to fulfill them. It's a never-ending cycle. Desires are artificially created in our minds, and we are in perpetual motion to fulfill them.

A man living two hundred years ago did not strive to buy a fancy car because there were no cars. He most probably just wanted a house and have sufficient food to survive and feel safe. He likely had fewer desires and experienced more internal peace (providing his basic needs had been met). Once your basic needs have been met it won't make you happier if you add more material goods to your life. You need different things to keep you fulfilled. Maslow's hierarchy of needs beautifully illustrates this idea. The basic needs are the two lowest tiers of the pyramid.

As you climb the hierarchy of needs, having met your basic needs, and you start feeling the need for internal peace, an understanding of your mind and how it interacts with the world around you is critically important. Trying to find peace of mind without investigating your diet and your media intake (your 'mental nutrition') is like trying to row a boat with the anchor still stuck in the ground. You can row all you want, but your desire to be spiritually connected will just be that, a desire.

A fundamental change of paradigm is required.

We have the power to disengage ourselves from this

media conditioning. Once I realized I was a soul traveling from life to life, I started looking at life differently. I thought to myself: "Why blindly follow what everybody else is doing? Most people seem completely conditioned by media and their environment and never investigate if these powerful currents will truly lead them to a happy state of being. They just assume it does, eventually." I started thinking in terms of freedom. Asking questions like: "What will truly make me free? What keeps me bound, life after life? What subconscious patterns am I perpetuating that keeps this never-ending cycle of birth and rebirth going? What constitutes true happiness? Is it material, mental, spiritual, or facets of all three?"

Trying to get spiritually connected therefore has everything to do with the way our mind acts and reacts with the world around us. When we continue to be heavily conditioned by the ways of the world, naturally a large part of our internal resources are dedicated to fulfilling worldly desires. There won't be much time and energy left to dedicate to internal growth. Our mind will also endlessly display restless waves. These waves are what stands in the way of a spiritual connection.

If you are totally unprepared you'll have to work through two layers of waves. The restless waves of your conscious mind are relatively easy to calm down. But the subconscious debris is what makes things more difficult. This is the deeper, and if you are unprepared, thicker layer. Some of the accounts of people in this book are those who have investigated life at a deeper level. They have made certain adjustments and life choices that helped them distance themselves from the crazy ways of the world. They have become aware of their subconscious tendencies and have mostly let go of external influences and their past.

Samskaras (Sanskrit for subconscious debris) are latent tendencies or impressions that linger in the subconscious mind. The density of these impressions is what determines the clarity of our connection with the superconscious reality. The denser these impressions, the harder it is to connect. The clearer the subconscious mind is, the easier it is to connect.

Earlier we defined three blocks to achieving a superconscious connection. The second and third blocks are intimately connected. The waves of our mind (second block) are intimately connected with our karma (third block).

The deeply rooted subconscious layers are not only the result of karma but that which perpetuates karma as well. Karma causes events in our lives and minds, to which we react, creating new karmas. Every action has a reaction, equal and opposite. Living without awareness is acting and reacting to the impulses of our own karma, which has determined the world we live in. It is responsible for our parents, our environment and our body.

We don't need to be passively subject to these karmic forces. If you are born randomly, merely the result of parental, environmental and genetic conditioning, then you wouldn't have any choice in the matter. But karma chooses these parents, this body and this environment to help you elevate yourself beyond them. The more conscious you become, the more you will be participating in the choice of the circumstances of your next birth.

But when you realize this set of circumstances is merely a dress you wear, a play you step into, then you have the power to undress or walk off stage. This is only possible when you look upon yourself as a soul, separate from your body and mind. You inhabit the body and mind, you are not the body and mind.

In order to elevate yourself beyond the karmic forces that seem to govern every aspect of your life, special techniques are required which I like to call yogic techniques. The basic premise is that when you regard yourself as a non-material soul, then you can look upon layers of subconscious debris as frequencies that are lower than your soul's frequency. These frequencies are wrapped around your soul like a sheath.

When you leave the body these sheaths of frequencies come with you. Until you are enlightened consciousness, these remain wrapped around your soul even in-between lives and come with you when you reincarnate. The best way to change a frequency is with another frequency. Very effective techniques for changing subconscious debris frequencies are mantras. Think of a woman opera singer shattering a wine glass merely by the power of her high pitched voice. The sound waves crush the molecular structure of the glass.

Mantras can shatter the density of your accumulated subconscious impressions. By consciously bombarding the subconscious mind with mantric sound waves we can clean up the mind.

Once we clean up the mind we manifest superconscious frequencies that are emitted by our own soul. The thinner the layers, the more soul power we will be able to manifest.

All it requires is a basic understanding of this concept and then for us to actually practice it. You'll only know the power of these techniques by practical experience. The proof is in the pudding, as they say.

Very effective, along with these mantras are breathing exercises. As we discussed in an earlier chapter, the breath, and the mind are intertwined. When the breath slows down, so will the waves of the mind. A traditional yogic method is to first do some gentle stretching (body), then do breathing exercises (mind) and then do your meditation (mind and karma). This three-pronged approach is very effective to calm down our nerves, clear the mind and burst karma. The result is a calmer state of mind, allowing us to connect more easily to the divine consciousness hidden in our own hearts and in the universe.

We all operate differently and have different preferences when it comes to meditation and connecting to Source energy. By no means do I suggest that the above method is the only or even best method. But it is one of the ways to connect to Source Energy if you are seeking and are unsure how to achieve it.

"Spiritual practice is not just sitting and meditating. Practice is looking, thinking, touching, drinking, eating and talking. Every act, every breath, and every step can be practice and can help us to become more ourselves."

Thich Nhat Hahn.

Daily, I am meeting beautiful souls that have developed their own way of meditation and over lifetimes have found unique and beautiful ways to connect to the divine. What matters is that we understand that we do not need to stand by and let karmic forces shape our lives. There are things we can do if we want to have quicker results establishing a better sense of divine communication. We can and need to do something about it.

Equally important as the preparation for an LBL session is the way you maintain your connection with divine consciousness after a session. Over and over again we hear the divine beings or the Council of wise ones advise the client to meditate. Meditate, meditate, meditate. The beauty and power of an LBL session lies in the power it has to open up communication with a higher aspect of your own Self which is a connection with the Divine Source as well. In order for this awareness to keep guiding you after the session divine maintenance is required.

A good way to keep up this connection is to do everything we have discussed in this chapter regarding preparation. Keep up practicing the same techniques used in the preparation. As long as you have your own divine routine you stay connected because it means you are aware of what matters. Your True North is clear and present and you are unlikely to drift off in forgetfulness of your true purpose on earth.

Living in a semi-conscious fog is what you want to avoid. You don't want to just be vegetating while spending your time of earth without really making progress towards the attainment of your eternal freedom.

When we forget, we are merely surviving. We work to maintain the body and entertain the mind. Forgotten that the only reason we stepped into and are using this body and mind is to work towards our enlightenment. This forgetfulness will lead us to have to be born over and over again, each time trying to survive, perpetuating the cycle. The Buddhist wheel of Dharma signifies this endless cycle of birth and death. Living in awareness means we have not forgotten. And every action we do is one way or another leading us closer and closer to our freedom.

Every bit of freedom we attain directly translates to a happier state of mind. The thinner the subconscious layers of debris become, the more powerfully will the infinite power of our own higher being shine through, and the more we will be able to experience this light shining within. We are the light. The most practical thing we could possibly do for ourselves is to manifest this light. The Kindom of God is truly within.

A traditional religious idea is that we qualify ourselves, when we live a good life, for a heavenly afterlife. But the most powerful realization that comes from seeing people enter these divine states of consciousness during the LBL sessions is not just that there is life after death, but that we are an eternal soul that is always free.

What we learn from the experiences of people in high states of consciousness is that heaven is not a place. It is not even a state after death, but a state of being, a frequency you have permanently plugged into.

Heaven is being free from the illusion that you are this body, and that this world that you see is the real and only world. Right here and now, when you enter a high state of consciousness, you could experience a completely different reality. That has nothing to do with whether you are alive or dead, in this world here or in the between-lives state. This experience can be had here and now.

The goal is not merely to be free once you leave this earth, but to be free irrespective of what dimension you are in. Happiness and freedom is a state of consciousness and can be felt within at every moment of the day.

The experiences of clients in the in-between life states are merely a reminder of what such a consciousness feels like once you detach from the body and the world this body exists in. The misconception is that we first need to leave the body to experience this. That is not true. It is true that the body and its dense frequency makes it much harder to experience such a state of superconsciousness. But we don't have to wait and die first.

We do yoga, we meditate, go to church or enter a mosque so that we may become closer to divine happiness. When we add to that certain practices, along with a proper understanding of reality, we can supercharge our current state of consciousness, developing a permanent state of happiness. Why not feel the Christ, Buddha or Krishna consciousness right now?

Whatever practice you may have, whatever tradition you may come from, these are all different paths leading up to the same mountain. But the view, once you are at the top of the mountain, above the clouds, is beyond description and equal for all of us. The paths may be different, but they lead us to the same goal.

As long as we are walking on our particular mountain path we are still wearing the masks of our background and conditioning. It's our diversity. But as we ascend on the mountain we shed mask after mask to realize that others too, coming from a different direction, are ascending the same mountain. And that once we meet at the top, after having lost all our masks, we embrace each other in unison, exuberant as we share the incredible view from this place high above the world below.

The task at hand is not to worry or be concerned about others and the path they choose. Our task is to figure out how best we can ascend with the tools we have and the obstacles we face. Many get stuck in the jungle below the foot of the mountain, and cannot even see there is a mountain due to the thickness of the forest foliage. The enlightened ones come down from the mountain to tell us about the view beyond and help us on our way. As we slowly ascend we too can love and guide others along the way, so that together the journey becomes easier and more enjoyable for all.

Bliss is here and now.

About the author

Pieter Elsen was born in Holland and has lived in 5 different countries and on 3 different continents. Born and educated in The Netherlands, Pieter studied 5 years at the renowned Design Academy in Eindhoven, specializing in Industrial Design. Though he graduated with honors, Pieter felt there was more to life and set out on a 20-year journey of Self Discovery that brought him to France, India, England and finally the United States.

Pieter was a Vedic monk for 21 years, of which 11 were spent in India. While there he studied extensively the deep and spiritual philosophy of the East. He uses this experience and knowledge as a therapist and life coach counselor integrating the Western and Eastern schools of thought.

After coming to the United States he channeled his experience as a gifted motivational speaker and background in philosophy and international cultural diversity into the field of Clinical Hypnotherapy. In 2014 Pieter attained his Ph.D. in Metaphysical Humanistic Science with specialties in Transpersonal and Spiritual Counseling.

Trained and accredited by The Newton Institute for Life-Between-Lives Hypnotherapy, Pieter specializes in 'past-life' and 'life-between-lives' spiritual regression, where he helps you to re-discover your true immortal Self. He conducts LBL sessions throughout the USA and abroad. To contact Pieter for a private past-life / life-between-lives session, workshops or speaking engagements, or to buy his books please visit:

www.elsenhypnotherapy.com
www.whensoulsawaken.com

or email:

elsenhypnotherapy@gmail.com

CPSIA information can be obtained
at www.ICGtesting.com
Printed in the USA
LVHW051613300423
745690LV00003B/115